· A HISTORY LOVER'S ·
GUIDE TO

ST. LOUIS

· A HISTORY LOVER'S ·
GUIDE TO

ST. LOUIS

Vicki Berger Erwin

VICKI BERGER ERWIN AND JAMES W. ERWIN

James W. Erwin

H
THE
History
PRESS

Published by The History Press
Charleston, SC
www.historypress.com

Front cover, top, left to right: *Apotheosis of St. Louis* statue at the St. Louis Art
Museum. Author photo; Fox Theatre. *St. Louis Landmarks;* Gateway Arch,
National Park Service; *bottom*: Old Courthouse, *National Park Service*.
Back cover: Bevo Mill, *Missouri Historical Society*.

First published 2023

Manufactured in the United States

ISBN 9781467151351

Library of Congress Control Number: 2022947089

Notice: The information in this book is true and complete to the best of our
knowledge. It is offered without guarantee on the part of the authors or The
History Press. The authors and The History Press disclaim all liability in
connection with the use of this book.

CONTENTS

CONTENTS

ACKNOWLEDGEMENTS

I t is a known fact that books don't write themselves. Fortunately, in the case of this book, we had people who helped us write it along the way. Among many others, we especially want to give our thanks to the following:

Dan Fuller at Bellefontaine Cemetery. for very informative tours of the cemetery and great stories about the people interred there.

Nick Sacco at the U.S. Grant National Historic Site (White Haven).

Hope Mabrey, former volunteer and intern services manager at Missouri History Museum, for arranging tours for volunteers at MHM of important historic sites in St. Louis.

Kat Bourek, current volunteer and intern services manager, for continuing to create tours for volunteers and helping us expand our knowledge of St. Louis history.

Tom Keay at Campbell House Museum, for a great tour and answering a multitude of questions.

Gwynneth Rausch at Chatillon-DeMenil House, for taking us through the mansion, including climbing up to the top of the house to show us the World's Fair Collection.

Chad Rhoad at The History Press, for coming up with great ideas for us to write about and guiding us on our way.

Rick Delaney at The History Press, for always making our manuscripts better.

INTRODUCTION

We love history and consider ourselves fortunate to live in St. Louis, where there is so much to explore. This book was different from anything we've written before, and it took us a while to figure out how to write it. It's something of a hybrid: a history of St. Louis, but also a guidebook to sites throughout the city that we hope will enhance readers' knowledge of the city and its history.

When we started this project, we had a lengthy list of the sites we wanted to include, but when we realized our historical starting point is ten thousand years ago, we quickly decided that we would have to be selective to avoid having the publisher put out an encyclopedia. We chose to cover the historical high points of each era (as we've arbitrarily divided time). And we chose locations that we believed to be good examples for a history lover, experienced or new to the subject, to visit. We realize we've left some things out that others might consider to be important and haven't written enough about some places and people that some would say deserve a fuller treatment. To them, we say go to these places. You will find more than we could ever include in one volume.

St. Louis is more than the city, at least in our estimation. We've expanded our definition of St. Louis to include sites we felt were important in its history, such as Imperial in Jefferson County, Cahokia Mounds in Illinois and St. Charles, all part of the metropolitan area.

One of the great joys of writing this book was visiting sites we hadn't seen before. We knew they were there and that we should go see them, and now we have. It was fun.

The places we have identified are historic or are museums that contain and explain history, but St. Louis' story is more than just its places. It is also about its people. We hope you enjoy the bits and pieces we included about some of the city's citizens.

You will find websites for the places we write about in the bibliography, but websites, online links and telephone numbers can and do change from time to time. We recommend that you do an online search for the places you want to visit to get current information about hours, special exhibits, events and directions.

Chapter 1

PREHISTORY

About 80,000 years ago, the earth's temperatures were so cool that sea level was about 150 feet lower than it is today. The sea reached its lowest level between 23,000 and 10,000 years ago. As a result, there stretched between modern Asia and North America a "land bridge" known as Beringia where the Bering Strait is now. Beringia was a broad plain extending nearly one thousand miles wide with its own flora and fauna. Man crossed Beringia 14,000 or more years ago to the North American continent.

The civilizations that preceded the arrival of Europeans are considered "prehistorical" because these peoples were nonliterate. Thus, our knowledge of them and their way of life is necessarily derived from inferences that may be drawn from the archaeological remains.

The earliest peoples, Paleo-Indians, were nomadic hunters who gradually transitioned to a hunting and foraging culture throughout the Missouri and Mississippi River valleys around ten thousand years ago. Clovis spear points and arrowheads from the earliest known of the Paleo-Indians have been found at Mastodon State Park associated with the bones of mastodons, giant ground sloths and peccaries.

The Mississippian culture began to emerge around AD 7850. It featured homes grouped around a courtyard; large, probably ceremonial structures; the appearance of chieftains; and the increased importance of corn as the primary crop. Around 1050, a city of fifteen thousand inhabitants—often called "America's First City"—suddenly appeared in the floodplain across from present-day St. Louis. We don't know what its residents named it, as they had no written language, but today we call it Cahokia Mounds. The name is a misnomer, coming from one of the subtribes of the Illini, who didn't occupy the area until three hundred years after Cahokia Mounds was abandoned.

The Mississippians at Cahokia Mounds had a complex agricultural society. They had well-defined social classes and engaged in elaborate rituals, featuring political and religious theater as well as human sacrifice. The rituals may have been sparked by a supernova that was visible during the daytime for twenty-three days and at night for over two years beginning in 1054. Its remnants comprise the Crab Nebula, visible in the night sky today.

We know the Mississippians at Cahokia Mounds were conversant with geometry, astronomy and calendars, as evidenced by the remains of circles of large wooden poles used to observe the summer and winter solstices. Archaeologists who studied them have dubbed the site "Woodhenge." Archaeologist Dr. Warren Wittry discovered the circles in 1961 while doing excavations in connection with the construction of Interstate 255.

The most remarkable features of this civilization are the numerous mounds that give the site its name. Cahokia had 120 mounds, 80 of which survive today. The largest is Monks Mound, named for the French Trappist monks who were the first Europeans to see the mounds in the 1700s. They built cabins and a chapel on its upper terrace. Monks Mound is 790 feet wide and 1,040 feet long. It has three terraces, built in stages. The highest is 100 feet above a fifty-acre Grand Plaza the size of thirty-five football fields. Monks Mound covers fourteen acres and has twenty-two million cubic feet of soil, all of which was hauled by hand in more than fourteen million basket loads.

In 1966, archaeologists discovered that the city had been surrounded by a stockade with guard towers that required an estimated twenty thousand trees for its construction. Excavations have uncovered burial pits with evidence that human sacrifices of young women were conducted. Among the artifacts uncovered were a collection of stone axes in discrete sets that *Archaeology Magazine* called a "cold, hard cache" that may have symbolized the "burying of the hatchet" by warring tribes.

By 1300, America's First City was abandoned and most of the inhabitants had left the Mississippi Valley. Where they went is still debated, but there are traces of Mississippian culture in numerous Plains tribes, including the Sioux, Pawnee, Osage, Omaha, Iowa, Missouria, Winnebago, Mandan and Crow.

The greatest number of mounds were in the Cahokia complex, but there were others nearby. St. Louis had forty-five mounds in and around the city, giving it at one time the nickname "Mound City." There were another twenty-six mounds in East St. Louis, Illinois. All of these mounds have been destroyed by construction. The last major mound in downtown St. Louis was the Big Mound. It was 319 feet long, 158 feet wide and 34 feet tall. Careless demolition destroyed priceless artifacts buried in the mound. The only evidence the Big Mound existed is a plaque at North Broadway and Mound Street, next to the Stan Musial Bridge. Sixteen mounds were excavated and destroyed in Forest Park as part of the construction of the 1904 World's Fair. Only one mound, Sugar Loaf Mound, remains in St. Louis. It is owned by the Osage Nation of Oklahoma.

Father Jacques Marquette is the first explorer to write about the area that became Missouri and St. Louis while traveling the Mississippi River. He learned of another river that joined the Mississippi from the Illini Indians, who called it *Pekitanoui*. Marquette's guides told him that the people who lived on this river were the *mihsoori* or *wemihsoori* ("people of the wood canoe"). Marquette wrote the name as *8emess8rit*. According to Michael Dickey, in seventeenth-century French script, the "8" was pronounced as a long "o." The word would have been pronounced "oo-emis-ooray." The "e" was later dropped by French mapmakers, and subsequently, the first syllable was dropped as well. Thus, the people became known as the Missouria, and the river, and ultimately the territory and state, became known as Missouri.

The Missouria nation was powerful in its day, numbering as many as ten thousand people at the height of its existence. None of the Native American tribes had permanent villages in present-day St. Louis, but many, such as the Missouria and the Osage, hunted in the region. When the French arrived, these tribes were frequent visitors to the new village as part of the fur trade that was St. Louis's first industry.

Mastodon State Historic Site

1050 Charles J. Becker Drive
Imperial, MO 63052

In 1839, Albert Koch owned a museum in St. Louis. He investigated reports of old bones emerging along the banks of Rock Creek near the city and found what he believed to be a new animal, the Missouri Leviathan. Creating a traveling exhibit, he displayed the bones in the United States and Europe. While he was in England, comparative anatomist Richard Owen convinced Koch that the bones weren't of a new animal but rather of an American mastodon.

At the turn of the twentieth century, C.W. Beehler, an amateur paleontologist, excavated skulls, jaws, teeth, tusks and fossils from the site. He set up a

The museum at Mastodon State Park has replicated what might have been seen in the area during the Paleo-Indian Clovis culture, when humans and mastodons coexisted. *Author photo.*

primitive museum and entertained visitors to the 1904 World's Fair with his finds. However, the finds were poorly documented and not accepted by the scientific community.

In subsequent years, the site was overrun by amateurs digging for bones, many of which were sold or removed. Further damage occurred from 1870 to 1930, when a quarry operated at the site.

The Works Progress Administration, a New Deal agency during the Depression, sponsored an archaeological excavation in 1940–42 by Robert McCormick Adams of the St. Louis Academy of Science. It found fossils but no artifacts.

The site was threatened by the construction of Interstate 55 in the 1970s, and this renewed interest in preserving the site. Grassroots efforts, including by local schoolchildren, raised enough money to buy 416 acres. The site was turned into a state park.

In the late 1970s and early 1980s, Missouri State Parks sponsored new archaeological investigations, yielding the first solid evidence that humans and mastodons coexisted in North America. A stone Clovis-type projectile was found with mastodon bones. The Clovis culture is the earliest well-documented Native American culture in North America. One theory suggests that their hunting practices may have contributed to the extinction of Pleistocene-era animals. Mastodon State Park is one of the oldest archaeological sites in Missouri (more than ten thousand years old) and is a rare example of stratified Ice Age Paleo-Indian Clovis culture.

The park features a museum with displays, artifacts, exhibits and a video that help the visitor understand the significance of the site. There is a replica of a mastodon skeleton that is a favorite with young and old visitors alike.

There are no current excavations at the site, and the remnants of previous digs are buried. However, there are three trails, including one to the Kimmswick Bone Bed, where the bones and artifacts were discovered.

Visitors may also take advantage of picnic facilities, a shelter and a playground and may view the wildflower garden.

Cahokia Mounds State Historic Site

30 Ramey Drive
Collinsville, IL 62234
The Cahokia Mounds State Historic Site Interpretive Center offers visitors orientation at its theater and exhibits. The interpretive center features re-creations of life and architecture at Cahokia during its heyday, based on the theories and discoveries of historians and archaeologists. (At this writing, the center is undergoing renovations and hopes to reopen by 2023.) There is also a reproduction of a Woodhenge circle, where one can, on the appropriate days, observe equinoxes and solstices.

Sugar Loaf Mound

4420 Ohio Street
St. Louis, MO 63111
The Sugar Loaf Mound, owned by the Osage Nation of Oklahoma, is the last remaining Indian mound in St. Louis and the oldest man-made structure in the city. It is approximately forty feet tall, one hundred feet long and seventy-five feet wide. There is no public access to the mound at this writing. The Osage did not build the mound but claim it as part of their heritage as descendants of the mound builders.

Chapter 2

DISCOVERY AND FOUNDING OF ST. LOUIS

THE FOUNDING OF ST. LOUIS

In the late summer of 1763, Pierre Laclède and his fourteen-year-old assistant, Auguste Chouteau, started upriver for Fort de Chartres near today's Prairie du Rocher, Illinois, with the aim of setting up a new post on the west side of the Mississippi River north of the fort. Before leaving New Orleans, Laclède learned that France had relinquished its North American claims to Canada and the area between the Mississippi River and the Appalachian Mountains under the treaty that concluded the French and Indian War. This made the new post even more important as a bulwark against the British. What Laclède did not know was that France had also turned over its claim to lands west of the Mississippi River to Spain.

Laclède's party reached Ste. Genevieve, the first permanent European settlement in Missouri, in December. That settlement was too far south of the Missouri River to suit his purposes. He, Chouteau and their men scouted the west bank for a more suitable spot. They found a gently sloping plateau above a bluff with access to fresh water and fields for laying out a town and cultivation of crops. Chouteau later recorded that Laclède marked three trees and told him, "You will come here as soon as navigation opens, and will cause this place to be cleared."

On February 14, 1764, Chouteau and twenty men landed at what is now St. Louis. They began to clear the site the next day. Laclède arrived in April and laid out the village. Chouteau recalled that Laclède "named it

Saint Louis, in honor of Louis XV, who[se] subject he expected to remain, for a long time. He never imagined he was subject to the King of Spain." Residents of Cahokia fled to St. Louis to escape British rule and became the first settlers, on lots assigned to them by Laclède. He also designated one lot for a church, where today the Old Cathedral stands, on the only parcel of St. Louis land that has not changed hands since its founding more than 250 years ago.

THE BATTLE OF ST. LOUIS: THE WESTERNMOST BATTLE OF THE REVOLUTIONARY WAR

When the thirteen American colonies rebelled against the British Crown in 1776 and Spain declared war on England in 1779, St. Louis leaders suddenly found themselves needing to defend the settlement. The hostilities had spilled from the Atlantic coast to the Illinois country west of the Appalachians. George Rogers Clark had already led expeditions against British troops and their Indian allies in the Ohio River valley.

The English asked Wabasha, a Dakota, and Matchekewis, an Ojibway, to lead a band of warriors to attack the Spanish settlement at St. Louis and the Americans at Cahokia. The chiefs gathered 750 Sioux, Chippewa, Menominee and Winnebago and about 200 reluctant Sauk and Fox at Prairie du Chien in what is now Wisconsin and headed south on May 2, 1780.

The lieutenant governor, Captain Fernando de Leyba, had been forewarned about the possibility of attack in March. He immediately ordered defensive measures. His men quickly constructed Fort San Carlos, a round stone tower forty feet tall, and armed it with five cannons. The tower was a shell, with a floor for the cannons but no roof. Leyba wanted four such towers, but there was neither time nor money to build them. He settled for entrenchments that extended from the tower to the river. He had 34 regular soldiers and 220 militia members to man the fortifications, augmented by another 150 men from Ste. Genevieve.

Wabasha's scouts approached the village on May 25, 1780. They couldn't get close to the fortifications without giving their position away, but the village seemed unconcerned about an attack. The fields outside the town were filled with women and children, picking strawberries and fruit for the Feast of Corpus Christi. The next day, Wabasha and Matchekewis attacked.

Leyba was still unprepared for the assault when it came. Civilians were in the fields and fled in terror to safety. Unfortunately, several were killed or captured. Leyba's men rushed to the tower and lobbed artillery rounds at the enemy. The Sauk and Fox contingent of Wabasha's little army retreated, not wanting to have come from the beginning; the others continued to fight. After unsuccessfully attempting to draw Leyba's defenders from the fort and trenches, Wabasha and Matchekewis retreated.

A simultaneous attack on Cahokia across the river was repulsed by the unexpected presence of some of George Rogers Clark's rangers. Twenty-one persons were killed in the battle, but St. Louis and possibly all of the Spanish lands claimed west of the Mississippi were saved from British rule. The Battle of St. Louis was the westernmost skirmish of the Revolutionary War.

The Old Cathedral

209 Walnut Street
St. Louis, MO 63102

What is commonly known as the Old Cathedral is officially the Basilica of St. Louis, King of France. When all of the surrounding buildings were demolished to make room for the Gateway Arch, the Old Cathedral was left intact. It was designed and built by Laveille and Morton, the first architecture firm west of the Mississippi River and north of New Orleans. The cathedral was consecrated and its first Mass conducted on October 26, 1834. Today, Mass is still performed in the cathedral, although it is a parish of personal choice rather than a territorial parish.

The Old Cathedral is closely tied to the early history of St. Louis and is considered the "mother church" of the city, as it is on the site of the first church. City founders Laclède and Chouteau set aside land west of Laclède's residence. It was one of three important "blocks": Cathedral Block, Public Square and Company Block. These formed the nucleus of the new village. Today, it is the only building that remains of the original settlement.

Until there was a structure, a tent served as the site of Mass, and services were held by an itinerant priest. On June 24, 1770, Reverend Pierre Gibault consecrated a log building for the parish, although there was no resident priest until 1811. Five of William Clark's children were baptized in the log church, as well as Jean Baptiste Charbonneau, son of Sacajawea.

In 1818, a brick church became the home for Catholic Mass. Bishop Louis William Valentine Dubourg was the resident priest, making his home in St. Louis since 1815. At the same time, the parish developed a cemetery where many of the founders of the city were buried. The bodies were moved to Bellefontaine

Cemetery sometime in the 1840s–50s. Adjoining the church, St. Louis Academy/College (now St. Louis University) was established in 1821.

Today, the Old Cathedral is a museum covering all periods of the church's history, as well as an active parish. Artifacts of the Archdiocese of St. Louis are on display in the basement. Displays include prayer books in different languages, correspondence and nativities dating to the late 1860s, among many other items.

Pope John XXIII designated the Cathedral of St. Louis a basilica on January 27, 1961. A cathedral is the seat of the bishop; a basilica is so designated by the pope because of its historical and spiritual significance.

In 1963, a significant renovation of the basilica was unveiled. The limestone exterior was repaired; windows were

The official name of the Old Cathedral is the Basilica of St. Louis, King of France. *St. Louis Landmarks.*

replaced and a window was uncovered behind the altar; steeple, roof and gutters were repaired; front doors were restored; and many interior upgrades were made.

The Greek Revival building is noted for its marble altars and artwork donated by Louis XVIII, King of France and Navarre that shows St. Louis venerating the Crown of Thorns. The facade of polished stone features a belfry above, an octagonal spire, a ball of gilded brass and a cross. The interior features pews from 1893, sacred art from Europe, the organ predating 1834 (mostly rebuilt) and marble statues of the saints.

Masses are said daily at the basilica, and it is a popular site for weddings. Tours are also available.

Fort San Carlos

Fourth Street and South Broadway (plaque)
Fourth and Walnut Streets (site)
St. Louis, MO 63101

The only evidence of the westernmost battle of the Revolutionary War is the marker at South Broadway and Walnut Street. *Author photo.*

A plaque commemorating the battle and the site of Fort San Carlos is on the grounds of the Hilton Ballpark Hotel at South Broadway and Walnut, one block west of its actual location at Fourth and Walnut. Each year on the anniversary of the battle, May 26, the Commemoration Committee for the Battle of Fort San Carlos holds a ceremony to remember the persons who died in the attack.

Chapter 3

ROAD TO STATEHOOD

Settlers from the United States trickled into Spanish Louisiana in the 1780s. The most prominent immigrants were the Boone family. Daniel Boone, a former Virginia legislator, Indian fighter and already legendary frontiersman, was experiencing hard times in Kentucky. Boone's son Morgan came to Upper Louisiana and, in a meeting with Lieutenant Governor Zenon Trudeau, accepted a generous land grant of prime farmland in today's St. Charles County. He left four slaves behind to build a cabin and returned to Kentucky to bring the family's large clan to their new home. In September 1799, they set out for St. Charles: Daniel; his wife, Rebecca; his sons, Morgan and Nathan; and his daughters, Susanna and Jemima; as well as Isaac Vanbibber and his family. Nathan could not leave behind the love of his life, Olive Vanbibber, and abruptly turned back to marry her. They joined the family later. Daniel was treated royally in his new home. He was received with honors in St. Louis by the Spanish lieutenant governor. After Rebecca died in 1813, Daniel moved in with Nathan, where he lived until his death in 1820.

The focus of the American government's interest in Spanish Louisiana was on keeping navigation open and free on the Mississippi River to New Orleans, the only outlet for goods to be exported or imported to the states and territories west of the Appalachians. In 1798, Spain allowed the "right of deposit" to American shippers—the right to land their goods pending shipment elsewhere.

In 1800, rumors circulated in Europe and Washington that Spain had agreed to retrocede to France the colony of Louisiana. The new American president, Thomas Jefferson, worried that transfer of control would bring the United States into conflict with the aggressive French Republic.

The Napoleonic Wars had ceased for a brief period in a fragile peace. The truce—for it was no more than that—allowed Napoleon to revive France's American colonial empire. Jefferson sent Robert R. Livingston to Paris to feel out the French and to find out whether Spain in fact had transferred Louisiana to France. If it had not yet happened, Livingston was to try to persuade the French not to go through with that part of the agreement with Spain. If the transfer had been agreed upon and could not or would not be rescinded, then Livingston was to seek the transfer of Florida to the United States.

In 1802, Spain terminated the right of deposit and denied Americans access to New Orleans, setting off alarm bells in the United States. Whether spurred by the withdrawal of the right of deposit or by rumors that the British had sent explorers to open up the Northwest to commercial exploitation, Jefferson approached his personal secretary, Captain Meriwether Lewis, to plan an expedition to the Pacific.

The dispute over the right to deposit increased the American desire to acquire Florida and New Orleans so that the Mississippi could be reopened to American shippers. Fortunately, the United States' urgency to satisfy its citizens in the West coincided with Bonaparte's decision to drop his dreams of a colonial empire in the New World. A renewal of the war between Britain and France was on the horizon, and France needed money. Napoleon authorized his ministers to ask whether the United States wished to acquire all of the French possessions on the North American continent. Livingston and James Monroe (who had been sent to assist the negotiations) leaped at the chance to buy all of Louisiana, even though they had no explicit authority to do so. They knew a good deal when they saw it, and there were worries that the French might change their mind. The news of the purchase soon reached Washington and was announced on July 4. Despite opposition from some New England members of Congress, the treaty was approved in October 1803.

The United States had vastly increased its territory, acquiring an area west of the Mississippi River stretching from the Gulf of Mexico to somewhere in the north and to somewhere in the west as far as the Rocky Mountains. The exact boundaries of the Louisiana Purchase were vague, as the treaty provided only that France was ceding to the United States whatever it had acquired from Spain. The price was $15 million (about $240 million in today's dollars). While it was a steep price for a government remarkable for its stinginess, it was still a bargain.

Spain did not actually transfer control of Louisiana to France in the three years after entry into the agreement between the two countries. It must have come as a shock to the residents of Upper Louisiana to learn that not only had the first transfer been made, but also that they were now to be the newest Americans. Their reaction was mixed. Many American settlers were apprehensive, as they feared (rightly so) that the new regime would bring with it new laws, new taxes, new customs and new cultural attitudes.

Jefferson appointed Captain Amos Stoddard, an artillery officer in the army, as the interim commandant of Upper Louisiana. Having taken no steps to assume control of Louisiana after acquiring the colony, the French had no one in St. Louis to transfer it. Captain Stoddard represented France in accepting the formal transfer from Spain on March 9, 1804. As a representative of the United States, he received the transfer from France on March 10.

LEWIS AND CLARK EXPEDITION

Lewis threw himself into both educational and logistical preparations once President Jefferson asked him to plan an expedition to the Pacific. Realizing he needed someone to help manage the day-to-day tasks, he wrote to an old army friend, William Clark, to see if he would be interested in joining the expedition as co-leader. A month later, Clark replied that he would "cheerfully join" Lewis.

Clark was the youngest brother of George Rogers Clark, whom Jefferson had sought to lead a similar expedition years earlier. William served with James Wilkinson while in the militia and joined the regular army in 1792. He fought at the Battle of Fallen Timbers in 1794 but resigned from the army due to poor health in 1796.

After months of gathering supplies, boats and men, Lewis and Clark finally arrived in St. Louis in time to witness Stoddard's receipt and transfer of the territory to the United States. It was too late to start the trip, because winter was coming on.

Clark led the enlisted men of the party to a campsite at Wood River, where they stayed while Lewis and Clark in St. Louis met important citizens. In May 1804, Clark came to lead them to St. Charles. There, they met

Meriwether Lewis for final preparations for the trip. Word of their arrival brought the sleepy village to life. Lewis was wined and dined by the elite of St. Charles, and his men took the opportunity for one last fling before setting off into the wilderness. The inhabitants gave a ball on Saturday night "which was attended by a number of the French ladies, who were remarkably fond of dancing." Some of the men enjoyed themselves a bit too enthusiastically, resulting in courts-martial and fines.

On May 21, 1804, the adventurers filled their vessels—a keelboat and two pirogues—with last-minute necessities. The party fired a salute from the swivel cannon and, giving the assembled inhabitants three cheers, set off for the unknown lands of the West at about three o'clock in the afternoon. The Corps of Discovery disappeared into the wilderness.

Two and a half years later, the party reappeared at St. Charles, where they were once again feted by the inhabitants. One member of the party, Sergeant John Ordway, noted in his journal that "we had been given out for dead above a year ago…the people of the Town gathered on the bank and could hardly believe that it was us for they had heard and had believed that we were all dead and were forgotton [*sic*]."

Lewis and Clark led their men to a heroes' welcome in St. Louis two days later. Ordway wrote in his journal:

> *About 12 oClock we arived in Site of St. Louis fired three Rounds as we approached the Town and landed oppocit the center of the Town, the people gathred on the Shore and Huzzared three cheers. we unloaded the canoes and carried the baggage all up to a Store house in Town. drew out the canoes then the party all considerable much rejoiced that we have the Expedition Completed and now we look for boarding in Town and wait for our Settlement and then we entend to return to our native homes to See our parents once more as we have been So long from them.*

ROSE PHILIPPINE DUCHESNE

In 1817, Bishop Louis Dubourg met Madeleine Sophie Barat, the mother superior of a recently founded religious community, the Society of the Sacred Heart of Jesus. One of her communicants, Rose Philippine Duchesne, "burned with the desire" to devote "her life for the salvation of the Indians." At Dubourg's request, the Sisters came to America to work in his diocese.

Despite hardships suffered during their first winter in the rude frontier community of St. Charles, the Sisters opened a school for girls in October 1818, the first free school west of the Mississippi River. It had only three paying students, daughters of two wealthy St. Louis families who boarded with them. Within a week, there were twenty-two neighborhood girls enrolled in the free school, who did not board. As for Blacks and mixed race students, the bishop "said positively that we may not admit them to either of our schools, and he had appointed one day a week to the instruction of the colored people; otherwise, he says, we should not hold the white children in school."

The Sisters were ordered to move the school to Florissant, and St. Charles was left without Sisters from the Society of the Sacred Heart for nearly ten years. Duchesne made a triumphant reentry into St. Charles in 1828 and reopened the school. It became the Academy of the Sacred Heart—still operating today on the same site.

Mother Duchesne also realized her dreams of ministering to young Indian students—to a point. The Jesuits asked the Sisters of the Sacred Heart to provide instruction to members of the Potawatomi tribe in eastern Kansas in 1841. Although seventy-one years old and frail, Mother Duchesne persuaded church authorities to send her along to "assure success to the mission by praying for us." She did not learn the language and so could not teach, but she made up for it by devoting long hours to prayer. To the Potawatomie children, she was known as Quahkahkanumad, or "Woman Who Prays Always."

Her health worsening, Mother Duchesne returned to St. Charles in 1842. She lived out the rest of her life in a small room under a stairway near the chapel at the school she helped to found. She served as an inspiration to other religious who stopped in St. Charles on their way west to receive her blessing. Rose Philippine Duchesne died on November 18, 1852, blind and feeble. She was canonized by Pope John Paul II in 1988. Her remains and artifacts from her life are in a shrine on the Academy of the Sacred Heart campus.

STATEHOOD FOR THE MISSOURI TERRITORY

In November 1818, the Missouri Territory formally sought the admission of Missouri as a state. From that time until 1821, the process proceeded on two tracks, one local and one national, which sparked a clash that became a rehearsal for civil war.

The forty-one delegates to the state convention elected to draft a constitution to submit to Congress for approval reflected the American elite of the territory. Most of the delegates were originally from Upper South states such as Virginia and Kentucky. Only two were of French heritage. The convention was dominated by what one wag called the "lawyer *junto*," because lawyers chaired seven of the eight committees chosen to write sections of the constitution.

In the meantime, Missouri's application for admission to the Union came before Congress. James Tallmadge, described by historian Robert Pierce Forbes as "a maverick single-term Republican congressman from Poughkeepsie," rose on February 13, 1819, to propose an amendment to Missouri's statehood bill providing "that the further introduction of slavery or involuntary servitude be prohibited…and that all children of slaves, born within the said state, after admission thereof to the Union, shall be free at the age of twenty-five years."

The debate that followed in the summer and fall of 1819 foreshadowed the controversies that arose in 1860, and the same arguments appeared: Pro-restrictionists argued that Congress had the power to prohibit slavery as a condition to admission to the Union, while proslavery advocates said that states were equals and thus Missouri could not be denied the right to have slavery when other states had it as well. Both sides deplored slavery as an "original sin" (an argument that would not be repeated in 1860), but southerners, including Thomas Jefferson, argued that the spread of slavery would ultimately make it less harsh—and besides, Blacks were better off as slaves than as free men and women. Pro-restrictionists pointed to the Declaration of Independence and the guarantee of republican government found in the U.S. Constitution. Both sides had difficulty reconciling the notion that "all men are created equal" with their social attitudes, but it was especially troubling to the defenders of slavery.

While this debate was ongoing, the Massachusetts legislature acquiesced to the long-standing desire of the District of Maine to become a separate state with one important condition: Congress had to pass such a bill before March 4, 1820. But a clear majority in the Senate opposed the admission of Maine if Congress was going to prohibit the admission of Missouri over the question of slavery.

Ultimately, the Missouri Compromise was reached, approving Missouri's southern border, the line of 36° 30′ latitude, as the northern boundary of new slave states (except, of course for Missouri). Maine was admitted to the United States on March 3, 1820. With the compromise on the 36° 30′

line and the admission of a Free State to correspond with the admission of Missouri as a slave state (thus preserving the political balance), it appeared that Missouri would become the twenty-first state.

But it was not to be. The Missouri Constitution was typical of the times, except for two provisions that caught objections from northern antislavery congressmen. The first prohibited free Blacks from entering the state, and the second prohibited the legislature from emancipating slaves unless owners consented. The dispute dragged on for another year until a Second Missouri Compromise was reached, with the state legislature promising not to pass a law forbidding free Blacks to travel to Missouri (a promise broken in 1845). Upon submission of this "solemn public act," President Monroe declared Missouri a state on August 10, 1821.

The Historic Daniel Boone Home at Lindenwood Park
1868 Highway F
Defiance, MO 63341

Although billed as the Historic Daniel Boone Home, this impressive stone building belonged to one of his sons, Nathan Boone. Daniel originally settled about four miles west of it.

When Daniel's wife, Rebecca, died in 1813, he moved in with his son. In 1816, Nathan and Daniel built a stone house on the banks of the Femme Osage Creek. Although tradition says Daniel made the pegged wooden doors, he likely supervised while Nathan did the hard work. And it was hard. He cut blue limestone into blocks three feet wide and weighing several hundred pounds and painstakingly dressed each one with a hammer and chisel. Once prepared, the stones were dragged by sled to the homesite. Using a block and tackle, Nathan set the blocks into the side of a hill overlooking the creek. When finished, the home had walls two and one-half feet thick, a full basement for the kitchen and dining room, two full floors above that and a large attic. The front had two full-length porches facing the creek. The first floor's windows doubled as gun ports with heavy shutters. The place was more than a home. It was a fort.

Daniel spent his final years in the magnificent home he and Nathan built, planning his funeral and enjoying his grandchildren. While waiting to die, Daniel ordered a Cherrywood coffin and placed it under his bed. He liked to show it off, and many visitors came to admire it. He was said to pull it out and take a nap in it, scaring the children. He was laid in it for the final time on September 26, 1820, when he died at the age of eighty-six.

Commonly called the Daniel Boone Home, the house belonged to Boone's son Nathan. Daniel lived here with his children during the years after his wife died and until his death. *Creative Commons.*

Today, the three-hundred-acre site also features historic buildings from the nearby area, including the Zephaniah Sappington/John Dressel Home, the Squire Boone Home, the Flanders Callaway Home, the Newton Howell Home, the Stake Home, the Benedict Warmbrodt Home, the schoolhouse, a carpenter's shop, a gristmill and the Old Peace Chapel.

Camp Dubois (Lewis and Clark State Historic Site)

1 Lewis and Clark Trail

Hartford, IL 62048

On December 12, 1803, William Clark wrote that he led the enlisted men of the Corps of Discovery to a campsite "nearly opposit the Missouries I came to in the mouth of a little River called Wood River, about 2 oClock and imediately after I had landed the N W wind which had been blowing all day increased to a Storm which was a ccompanied by Hail & Snow, & the wind Continued to blow from the Same point with violence." The men spent the next five months at Camp Dubois preparing for the expedition.

The original site at the mouth of Wood River no longer exists. With the drastic changes in the course of the Missouri River, the actual location of the camp is now in St. Charles County on the western side of the river. But at the current mouth of Wood River stands the Lewis and Clark Historic Site. Its interpretive center's exhibits include a full-sized reproduction of the keelboat used on the expedition. The cutaway boat shows the interior. There is also a reconstructed replica of the Camp Dubois Fort with five bunkhouses and Clark's cabin.

Lewis and Clark Boat House and Nature Center

1050 South Riverside Drive
St. Charles, MO 63301

Besides serving as Missouri's first state capital, St. Charles is known for being where Lewis and Clark began their historic voyage of discovery. The men and their journey are showcased at the Lewis and Clark Boat House and Nature Center on the riverfront. The displays in the museum tell the story of the Lewis and Clark expedition and include displays on geology, indigenous cultures and mapping. Replicas of the keelboat, red pirogue, white pirogue and dugout canoes are on display on the ground floor. Surrounding the building is a walk with plant life from the early 1800s. Don't miss the panoramic views of the Missouri River from the second-floor window.

Fort Belle Fontaine

13002 Bellefontaine Road
St. Louis, MO 63138

Fort Belle Fontaine was established in 1805 about twenty miles north of St. Louis. It was the first American military installation west of the Mississippi River. The original site was on the south bank of the Missouri River, but the channel of the river moved south during one of its floods, necessitating moving the fort to the bluffs at its present location in 1811. The fort functioned primarily as a "factory" (the early nineteenth-century name for a trading post) for selling and buying goods from Native Americans and trappers. Authorities soon decided the location was too far from the Osage Nation, the principal tribe that traded with St. Louis. George Sibley established Fort Osage in western Missouri, and it became the principal factory on the Missouri River. The fort remained a military post but was abandoned after the construction of Jefferson Barracks in 1826. It is now a 305-acre park administered by St. Louis County. It is listed in the National Register of Historic Places.

Shrine of St. Rose Philippine Duchesne

619 North Second Street
St. Charles, MO 63301

The shrine is a tribute and memorial to St. Rose Philippine Duchesne, who for thirty-five years served God by establishing schools in Missouri and Louisiana, establishing a novitiate for the Society of the Sacred Heart, ministering to Native Americans and praying.

When she died, Mother Duchesne was buried on the grounds of the Sacred Heart Academy that she founded. When her body was exhumed three years later, it was miraculously intact and then interred in a crypt with an octagonal shrine in front of the school. When Mother Duchesne was beatified in 1940, Rome decreed that her remains be interred indoors. In 1949, they were place in a marble sarcophagus in the old "back porch" of the original convent.

The shrine was begun in 1951; in 1952, the sarcophagus was moved into it. Originally a freestanding building, it was connected to the academy in 1961. It is, according to the original plan, unfinished.

The sanctuary of the shrine's modern interior is furnished with granite, reflecting Mother Duchesne's hard pioneer life. There are also relics of the saint's early days in St. Charles and a crucifix that hung in the convent St. Philippine attended in France.

The original 1818 school no longer exists, but visitors may see the parlors of the early convent building and the cell where Saint Rose Philippine Duchesne (America's fourth saint) died. Artifacts she brought from France are also in the archives, along with many original documents pertaining to the history of the school.

Chapter 4

STATEHOOD TO CIVIL WAR

THE FIRST STATE CAPITAL

After Congress initially approved the admission of Missouri as a state in March 1820, voters elected the first state officers and representatives in August. The General Assembly convened in St. Louis on September 18, 1820.

Surprisingly, the most contentious issue before the legislators was selection of the temporary seat of government. Sectional interests delayed the decision for weeks. Indeed, the General Assembly debated or voted on this question on sixty-six of its eighty-six days in session. After considering and rejecting ten candidates—some of them multiple times—the legislators compromised on St. Charles, making it the temporary capital of the State of Missouri.

After the special session in which the General Assembly passed a "solemn public act" ostensibly approving the Second Missouri Compromise and the president's declaration that Missouri was finally a full-fledged state, new elections were held in the summer of 1821. The forty-three members of the new state's legislature gathered in St. Charles in November 1821 for its first regular session in the upper floor of Charles and Ruloff Peck's General Store. Many of the new legislators came from frontier areas of the state. They dressed accordingly, in homespun clothes, buckskin leggings and hunting shirts. Governor Alexander McNair, however, as befitting his position, arrived in a fashionable beaver hat and swallow-tail coat.

The members' conduct could be as rough as their dress. Arguments on the floor occasionally sparked fisticuffs. One day, Andrew McGirk and Duff

Green got into a quarrel so heated that McGirk threw a pewter inkstand at Green. The two came to blows. When Governor McNair attempted to stop the fistfight by grabbing Green, another legislator pushed McNair aside and said: "Stand back, Governor, you are no more in a fight than any other man. I know that much law. I am at home in this business. Give it to him, Duff!"

State officials needed permanent residences in St. Charles, because the state constitution required them to live in the capital city. Governor McNair lived in a stone house at what is now 701 North Second Street that had been the home of Jean Baptiste Point du Sable, a Black man reputed to be the founder of Chicago. (The building is no longer there.) Secretary of State William G. Pettus found the capitol quarters too crowded for his duties and moved into a house (now 307 South Main Street) across the street and a few doors south of Peck's Store.

In 1826, St. Charles lost its state capital designation to the new permanent capital in Jefferson City. The state moved all of its "laws, journals, records, public documents and furniture" to the new location. William Pettus gave a farewell party at his home for the state officials who would also have to find new homes in the middle of the state. Pettus remained in St. Charles. Thus, the town that for five years "flourished and promised to be a place of very great importance" gave up its most prominent citizens.

FURS, TRAILS AND STEAMBOATS

The promising economic outlook for St. Louis and Missouri that stimulated the desire for statehood in 1819 and 1820 gave way to disease and depression in 1821. The City of St. Louis was legally chartered in 1822 and extended its boundaries to Seventh Street, but its population dropped by one-third.

The fur trade had been an important part of the St. Louis economy, making up 30 percent of its income. But it became even more important as the city marched into the 1820s. The economy recovered by 1824, helped by an expansion of the fur trade into the Upper Missouri River and the western slopes of the Rocky Mountains. Over six hundred trappers worked in the Rockies by the 1830s, many of them remaining even through the winters, earning them the nickname "mountain men." Entrepreneurs who owned the fur companies earned enormous profits. William Ashley, for example, created a personal fortune by marking up his products by as much as 2,000 percent.

At the same time, St. Louis became a base for trade with the Southwest. After Mexico gained its independence from Spain in 1821, the previously dangerous and illegal trade with Santa Fe and New Mexico was now legal. Santa Fe not only became an important point to sell goods, it also paid for them in silver—up to $200,000 a year in hard currency, an extremely scarce commodity in St. Louis in the early nineteenth century. Merchants such as Robert Campbell organized companies to take advantage of this boon. Acceding to the demands of Missouri politicians such as Senator Thomas Hart Benton, who recognized a need for a "highway" to the Southwest, the federal government commissioned George Sibley to survey and mark the Santa Fe Trail.

In 1817, the first steamboat, the *Zebulon Pike,* arrived on the St. Louis riverfront. In 1827, 259 steamboats landed regularly on the levee. It was the beginning of an enormous expansion of the steamboat trade. By 1840, St. Louis was the second-largest inland port on the western rivers after New Orleans. There were 573 steamboat landings in 1833, 1355 in 1836, and 189 steamboats made 1,928 landings in 1841. St. Louis ruled as the center of steamboat trade on the Upper Mississippi River and the Missouri River. Carondelet, downstream from St. Louis, became an important shipyard, constructing steamboats to ply the Mississippi and Missouri Rivers.

There were problems on the riverfront, however. By the mid-1830s, silt built up downstream from the levee, threatening to block access to it. In 1837, a young engineer from the U.S. Army came up with a plan to dump rocks into the river at strategic points in order to direct the current in a way to wash away the silt and save the port. His name was Robert E. Lee. Lee's project successfully, but only temporarily, forestalled the incipient disaster. The problem was not fully remedied until 1854, when another Civil War general, Samuel R. Curtis, completed construction that compressed the channel to scour the shore next to St. Louis and made it suitable for the landing of even the largest steamboats.

Another problem with the levee was that it had become more than five miles of mud, merchandise and filth. Warehouses crowded so close that it was difficult to reach the city beyond Front Street (the first street next to the levee). Only nine-tenths of a mile of the levee was paved at the height of the steamboat era in the 1850s. Dozens of steamboats tied up on the landing at one time, making them susceptible to fire and (in the winter) ice floes that could crush them together.

A YOUNG ARMY OFFICER COMES TO TOWN

In 1843, Second Lieutenant Ulysses S. Grant graduated from West Point and was stationed at Jefferson Barracks, south of St. Louis. His friend and West Point roommate, Frederick T. Dent, invited Grant to the family farm at White Haven, a few miles away. There Grant met Frederick's sister Julia. They were smitten with each other. Grant visited White Haven regularly to court Julia. The army interrupted the courtship by a transfer of Grant to Louisiana followed by his involvement in the war with Mexico. When Ulysses returned after having distinguished himself, he and Julia wed in 1848.

Grant remained in the U.S. Army until 1854, serving in California and Oregon. Julia remained at White Haven with their children. After his resignation, Grant joined Julia and lived with her family at the farm until Julia's father gave the couple eighty acres about one-quarter mile north of White Haven (the site of present-day St. Paul's Cemetery on Rock Hill Road), where Grant farmed and built a home they called Hardscrabble. They only lived in the house for three months and moved back to White Haven when Julia's mother died. In 1859, the Grants moved to St. Louis in "a neat little house…which was simply but comfortably furnished" at 1008 Barton Street. The family moved to Galena, Illinois, in 1860. The next year, Grant was appointed colonel of an Illinois infantry regiment. Missouri saw the beginning of Grant's climb to fame as a military commander during the Civil War when he served at Mexico, Ironton and Belmont. By February 1862, "Unconditional Surrender" Grant was a household name in the North.

DISEASE AND DISASTERS

In one of St. Louis's worst years, the city was pummeled by disease and fire. On January 2, 1849, two steamboats arrived in St. Louis with 66 passengers suffering from cholera. On January 6, the first St. Louisan died from the disease. Steamboats brought a steady flow of new people into St. Louis, including many "49ers" on their way to California to find gold. The disease spread easily in the close confines of a steamboat and continued to spread when someone who was sick or someone who left the boat not knowing they were sick entered the city's population. Officially, 4,317 persons died of cholera that year—unofficially, the total was much higher. It was estimated that 10 percent of the population were victims of the disease.

That was just the beginning of the troubles to afflict the city. On May 17, 1849, a fire of unknown origin began on the steamboat *White Cloud* moored at the north end of the levee. It spread quickly to other boats jammed together. A strong wind carried cinders toward the shore, settling on barrels of lard and bacon, bales of hemp and piles of wood and setting them ablaze. They burst into flames, turning the levee into a raging inferno that burned for eleven hours. Fifteen city blocks were destroyed, including 280 businesses, 430 buildings and twenty-three steamboats, and taking an unknown number of lives. The damage covered most of the area now occupied by the Gateway Arch National Park. The fire approached but did not consume the Old Cathedral. The total loss was estimated to be between $3.5 million and $6.0 million ($100 to $170 million in today's terms).

DRED AND HARRIET SCOTT

As befitting an ambitious and expanding city and county, St. Louis County built a new brick courthouse in 1828. By the time it was completed in 1832, the need for more space already made it inadequate. A new structure that incorporated the old courthouse as one wing was completed in 1839. It would house the trials of one of the most important legal cases in the country's history.

All Dred Scott wanted was freedom for himself; his wife, Harriet; and their two children, Eliza and Lizzie. After his owner, Dr. John Emerson, was appointed an assistant surgeon in the U.S. Army, he was assigned to Fort Armstrong in Illinois. He took Scott with him to Illinois, a Free State, and later to Fort Snelling, located near present-day St. Paul, Minnesota. Fort Snelling was in territory that was part of the Louisiana Purchase and free by virtue of the Missouri Compromise.

While at Fort Snelling, Scott met and married Harriet Robinson, a slave owned by Indian agent Major Lawrence Taliaferro. (Unlike most slave marriages, which were common law or slave custom affairs, the Scotts were legally married by the justice of the peace, her owner, Major Taliaferro.) Emerson returned to St. Louis and married Irene Sanford.

Emerson returned to Fort Snelling with his new wife and the Scotts, was later transferred to Florida and eventually left the military. Dr. Emerson died in December 1843, leaving Dred, Harriet and their children to Irene.

On April 6, 1846, Dred and Harriet Scott filed suit in the St. Louis Circuit Court seeking freedom from Irene Emerson's ownership, launching a decade-long saga. Under the facts and under Missouri law as it stood in 1846, the Scotts had a strong case. The Missouri Supreme Court had decided a case that was virtually identical several years before, holding that when a slave was taken to a Free State or territory to live, they were deemed to have been freed by operation of law. This principle applied even if the slave's owner was a military man compelled by orders to go to the Free State.

The first trial ended in a verdict for Emerson when the Scotts' lawyer failed to call any witness who could testify from personal knowledge that Irene Emerson owned Dred Scott, making him a slave. As historian Don Fehrenbacher points out, Emerson was able to keep the Scotts as slaves because there was no proof that they were her slaves!

The court cured this oversight by promptly granting a new trial. Emerson's lawyers appealed to the Missouri Supreme Court. The appeal was unsuccessful, but it ran two more years off the clock. At the second trial, the jury returned a verdict for the Scotts. Emerson appealed again.

The Scott family was swept up in a swirl of slavery politics that doomed their cause. Emerson's appeal languished in the Missouri Supreme Court until 1852, and the wait almost assured her of victory. On March 22, 1852, the court reversed the judgment of the circuit court granting the Scotts' freedom. The court overruled decades of precedent that held that slaves taken to live in Free States or territories for more than a brief sojourn were free by operation of law. One of the judges, Hamilton Gamble (later the wartime governor of Missouri), dissented on the grounds that Missouri precedent should not be overruled. "Times may have changed, public feeling may have changed, but principles have not and do not change, and in my judgment there can be no safe basis for judicial decisions, but in those principles which are immutable."

Scott's new attorney, Roswell Field (father of poet Eugene), decided not to seek review of the decision by the United States Supreme Court but filed suit in federal court seeking their freedom. The case was heard in the same courthouse because there was no separate federal court building at the time. The defendant this time was Irene's brother John Sanford. Irene had remarried and moved to Massachusetts. While he did not own the Scotts, Sanford held them on behalf of his sister, which was enough to make him a proper defendant under the law.

Unlike the prior two trials in state court, Field took no chance that witnesses might say something that would screw up the chance for a definitive ruling by filing an agreed statement of facts. The jury returned a verdict in favor of Sanford: Dred Scott and his family were not free because of their prior residence in Illinois and Minnesota.

The case reached the U.S. Supreme Court in December 1854. And there it languished once again, until February 1856. The parties in *Dred Scott v. John Sandford* (somebody misspelled Mr. Sanford's name in the court records, and it stuck for all time) argued the case for four days. And even that was not enough, for the court brought them back in December 1856 for twelve more hours of argument over another four days.

The heated political atmosphere of the slavery controversy in Missouri cost Dred Scott a victory in the Missouri Supreme Court. The same happened on the national stage. By the time a decision was reached, Congress had passed the controversial Kansas-Nebraska Act, repealing the Missouri Compromise and allowing states to decide for themselves whether or not to allow slavery.

On March 6, 1857, the justices of the Supreme Court gathered to issue their opinions in the case that would decide whether Dred Scott was a free man or a slave. Chief Justice Roger Taney delivered the opinion of the court. Taney droned on for two hours, reading his opinion in a barely audible monotone. Two other justices read their concurrences. The next day, the two dissenting justices read their opinions in proceedings that took a total of five hours. Despite the intense public interest, the court did not release the full text of the opinion. Indeed, all the public had (and all historians have of those two days) were newspaper reports. The failure of the court to make public an authoritative text of Taney's opinion was a scandal. One of the dissenting justices asked the clerk of the court for a copy of the opinion and was refused access to it. He suspected that Taney was revising to answer criticisms in the dissents (he was right). The written majority opinion was not made public until almost three months after it was delivered orally.

It was a complete and utter defeat for Dred Scott and those who, by now mostly members of the newly formed Republican Party, hoped the court would allow congressional restrictions on slavery. Taney held that African Americans were not citizens and had no right to bring lawsuits in federal court. As he said in a famously nasty phrase, "Negroes have no rights a white man is bound to respect." Taney continued, saying that Congress did not have the power to prohibit slavery in the territories, and thus the Missouri Compromise was unconstitutional. Therefore, Scott could not rely on his residence at Fort Snelling as a basis for his freedom. As for his residence in the Free State of Illinois, whether that was sufficient was a matter of Missouri law, and the highest court in that state had ruled against him.

Southerners praised the decision, because it adopted every principle they had argued for during the prior decade. Northerners condemned it. They argued that a majority of the justices did not agree with Taney on the issues of Negro citizenship and the Missouri Compromise and that Taney's opinion was merely *obiter dictum* (reasoning not necessary to the decision). The Latin phrase entered the public consciousness and became a curse word in some circles.

The nation had taken another step toward civil war.

John Sanford, the winning party, died on May 5, 1857. Irene and her family executed a quitclaim deed to Taylor Blow for the purpose of allowing Blow to free the Scott family. Blow signed the deed of manumission on May 26, 1857. Dred Scott died in 1858 and was buried in Wesleyan Cemetery, near Lindell Grove on the western edge of St. Louis. His remains were moved to Calvary Cemetery in St. Louis in 1867. Harriet Scott died in 1876 and was buried in Greenwood Cemetery in St. Louis County.

THE CIVIL WAR

Although a slave state, Missouri was not prepared to secede from the Union even if Abraham Lincoln won the presidential election of 1860. In the election, Lincoln won only 10 percent of the Missouri vote—mostly from St. Louis, where there was a substantial and strong antislavery German immigrant population.

Missouri did elect Claiborne Fox Jackson, a former Border Ruffian, as governor. Jackson favored secession and secretly took steps to bring Missouri into the Confederate States of America. He coveted the United States Arsenal at St. Louis. It held 60,000 muskets, 90,000 pounds of powder, 1.5 million ball cartridges, 40 cannons and machinery to manufacture weapons. Much of the early military and political maneuvering in Missouri centered on gaining control of the arsenal's weapons and ammunition.

Frank Blair Jr., a U.S. congressman and brother of Lincoln's postmaster general, was determined to hold the arsenal for the Union. He organized the "Home Guards," mostly German American immigrants in St. Louis, to counter secessionist "Minute Men." He also successfully had Captain Nathaniel Lyon, a staunch abolitionist, transferred to St. Louis to take command of the arsenal.

In the meantime, Jackson asked for and received from the legislature a call for a convention to consider secession on March 4. To Jackson's surprise and dismay, the convention voted overwhelmingly against secession. Missouri wanted to stay in the Union, to keep slavery and to avoid war. Nonetheless, war came on April 12, 1861. Governor Jackson condemned Lincoln's call for seventy-five thousand volunteers as "illegal, unconstitutional and revolutionary...inhuman and diabolical." Blair mustered his Home Guards into federal service, and Lyon had those men available to him in addition to the regulars stationed at the U.S. Arsenal.

Governor Jackson ordered the commander of the Missouri State Militia, Daniel Frost, to gather a force near St. Louis for "training." Frost assembled nine hundred men at "Camp Jackson" in Lindell's Grove (now the site of St. Louis University, then outside of the city).

Lyon suspected that Jackson and Frost intended to take the U.S. Arsenal. He stationed men on the hill above the arsenal (now Lyon Park) to ensure that Frost's men could not command the area. On May 10, with some 6,500 men, mostly German Americans from Blair's former Home Guards, Lyon surrounded Camp Jackson and demanded its surrender. Frost, knowing he could not defend against such an overwhelming force, gave up without a fight. But while Lyon's troops were marching the prisoners to town, they passed a crowd of civilians (including, among others William T. Sherman). Someone fired a gun. A soldier? A civilian? No one knows. The German troops, thinking a secessionist throng was shooting at them, fired into spectators. Before the melee was over, 28 persons were killed. Lyon took the prisoners to the arsenal, where they were paroled. The Camp Jackson Affair, as it became known, was the spark that ignited a bitter war among Missourians, including a guerrilla war that escalated from the burning of bridges to murders that left scars that never fully healed.

St. Louis quickly became the center of Union military operations on the Mississippi River. Benton Barracks (at the site of present-day Fairgrounds Park) was a major training center for Union regiments from Missouri, Illinois, Iowa, Minnesota and Wisconsin. In 1863–64, several regiments of the United States Colored Infantry were recruited and trained there. Fourteen new hospitals opened in St. Louis during the war to serve the sick and wounded.

James B. Eads built ironclads for the Union navy at Carondelet, and numerous steamboats were chartered or sometimes commandeered to transport troops and supplies to the Union armies fighting on and near the Mississippi.

St. Louis housed several prisons for Confederate prisoners of war, suspected sympathizers and convicted guerrillas and spies. The largest was the Gratiot Street Prison, which held up to two thousand persons in the former McDowell Medical College at Eighth and Gratiot Streets. (The building no longer stands, and Eighth Street at that location no longer exists; it is now the site of the Nestlé-Purina office complex.) The Union army converted former slave pens to prisons, most notoriously the Lynch's Slave Pen, which was renamed the Myrtle Street Prison. Before the war, Lynch's Slave Pen held slaves waiting to be sold, many of them on the eastern steps of the courthouse, just a block north on Broadway. Today, Busch Stadium and Ballpark Village are located on that site.

The period from 1820, when Missouri became a state, and the Civil War is a time when St. Louis grew and changed in many ways. It is also the period that offers a feast of restored sites to learn about the city's history.

First Missouri State Capitol Historic Site

200 South Main Street
St. Charles, MO 63301

St. Charles was never meant to be the permanent state capital of Missouri. Rather, Missouri was initially governed in two rented, adjoining spaces above a general store run by Charles and Ruloff Peck and a carpenter house run by Chauncey Shepard. The second-floor housed spaces necessary for state business: the House, the Senate, the governor's office and a small committee room. After the capital moved to its permanent site, the "First State Capitol" returned to its original use.

The legislators at the time were a rough and tumble, uneducated bunch. Physical fights often broke out on the floors of both House and Senate. Tobacco juice stained the floors and even dripped onto the spaces below. The rule was "spit where you sit." When the historic space was restored, floorboards had to be cleaned and, in some instances, replaced.

After housing many businesses through the years, the former state capitol building was boarded up as it deteriorated. A group of interested citizens convinced the State of Missouri to purchase it in 1960 and restore the building. Today, it is a Missouri State Park open for visitors. In addition to the historic site, there is an interpretive center adjacent to the capitol buildings.

The buildings are furnished in 1820s style. As it was in the days of the state capitol, the second floor is set up as legislative chambers, with only a door separating the House and the Senate. Half of the ground floor is a replica of Peck's Store, and the remainder is set up as the Peck family's home would have looked.

Restoration of the First State Capitol led to the renewal and preservation of what is now referred to as Historic Main Street, the largest historic shopping district in the state. The street features charming shops, restaurants and places to stay housed in restored, historic buildings.

Missouri's First State Capitol is now maintained by the State of Missouri. It is located in the heart of historic Main Street in St. Charles. *Missouri State Parks.*

The St. Charles County Historical Society is located near the former capitol building at 101 South Main in the Old Market House. It is in what has served as a Market and Fish House in the 1830s and later as St. Charles City Hall and Police Station. It is a depository for information on St. Charles City and County. There is also a small museum with rotating exhibits.

Many of the buildings on Main Street have stories to tell. For example, in 1837, Elijah Lovejoy, publisher of the antislavery newspaper the *St. Louis Observer*, visited St. Charles to speak to a church group. Lovejoy was married to the niece of Seth Millington, who owned the building on the corner of what is now First Capitol Drive and Main Street. After finishing the speech and returning to the Millington home, Lovejoy had to escape an angry proslavery mob. He was not so fortunate later, as he was murdered by a similar mob in Alton, Illinois. The Western House at 1001 South Main served as a stopping place for many travelers to the West. It was also a stagecoach stop and offered stabling and blacksmith services in the 1800s. Don Carlos Tayon, the second commandant of St. Charles, resided at 119 McDonough Street. Lewis and Clark are reputed to have visited and dined at the residence before their historic journey.

Jefferson Barracks

2900 Sheridan Road
St. Louis, MO 63125

Jefferson Barracks was opened in 1826 to replace Fort Belle Fontaine. It is the oldest operating military base west of the Mississippi River. It served the active-duty United States Army from 1826 to 1946. Future generals Ulysses Grant,

William Sherman, Robert E. Lee and James Longstreet were stationed here prior to the Civil War. President Zachary Taylor and his son-in-law, Confederate president Jefferson Davis (Taylor's daughter Sarah was Davis's first wife), were stationed here during part of their military careers. It is currently a base for the U.S. Army National Guard and Air National Guard. Encompassed within its grounds and its environs are the Jefferson Barracks National Cemetery, a U.S. Veterans Hospital, the Missouri Civil War Museum, the St. Louis County Jefferson Barracks Park, the Old Ordnance Room Museum, the Powder Magazine Museum, the Jefferson Barracks POW-MIA Museum and the Telephone Museum.

Jefferson Barracks is the oldest operating military base west of the Mississippi River and home to a large national cemetery. *Author photo.*

Jefferson Barracks National Cemetery

Although not formally created until 1866, the cemetery saw its first burial on August 5, 1827, when Elizabeth Ann Lash, the infant daughter of an officer stationed at Jefferson Barracks, was interred on the site. Of the 20,000 burials in the old section of the cemetery, Union dead were interred in sections by state, as far as that could be determined, including 7,536 white soldiers, 1,067 African Americans, 1,010 Confederate POWs and 556 persons "not of military service." In 1869, the remains of soldiers buried at other locations around the state were reinterred, as well as victims of smallpox who had been buried on Arsenal Island in the nearby Mississippi River. In 1939, the remains of 175 members of the Fifty-Sixth United States Colored Infantry who died of cholera in 1866 while returning from Arkansas to be mustered out were removed from their original burial place and reinterred at Jefferson Barracks.

There are a number of monuments throughout the cemetery, including to the Unknown Dead of 1861–65, to Merchant Marine Seamen and Navy Armed Guard and to those Who Served & Sacrificed within the Khe Sanh, Vietnam region. There is also the U.S. Submarine Veteran's Memorial and memorials to the U.S. Army's Third Infantry Division, the U.S. Army's Eighty-Second Airborne Division and the Fourth Marine Division.

There are eight Medal of Honor awardees buried in Jefferson Barracks National Cemetery. Other notable persons buried in the cemetery include Jack Buck, longtime St. Louis Cardinals radio and television announcer; Johnnie Johnson, pioneer rock musician; and Michael Blassie, the Vietnam Unknown Soldier until his remains were identified through DNA testing in 1998. There are 3,255 unknowns buried in the cemetery. There are currently about 237,000 persons interred at Jefferson Barracks. It remains an active cemetery with about twenty burials per day.

Old Ordnance Room Museum
345 North Road

The Old Ordnance Room Museum is owned and operated by St. Louis County Parks. It was built in 1851 as one of two limestone buildings to store gunpowder. It has temporary exhibits with military themes.

Powder Magazine Room Museum
535 Bagby Road

The Powder Magazine Room Museum is also owned and operated by St. Louis County Parks. It is a limestone building constructed in 1857. It has four-foot-thick walls, a wood floor and an arched ceiling. If the gunpowder stored in it exploded, the force would blow through the floor and the arches would collapse on the debris, smothering the fire. The walls and roof would remain. At least, that was the theory. It was never tested. Exhibits in this museum cover the history of Jefferson Barracks.

Missouri Civil War Museum
223 Worth Road

The Missouri Civil War Museum opened in 2013 in the former Post Exchange and Gymnasium buildings. It includes not only a museum space with numerous exhibits related to the Civil War in Missouri but also a separate event space,

The Missouri Civil War Museum is located on the grounds of Jefferson Barracks in what was at one time the Post Exchange and Gymnasium. *Author photo.*

a library and the most complete Civil War bookstore and gift shop in the metropolitan area.

Jefferson Barracks POW-MIA Museum
16–18 Hancock Avenue
The Jefferson Barracks POW-MIA Museum was organized in 2011 to honor members of all branches of the military who were captured or who remain missing in action in any year and in any conflict.

Jefferson Barracks Telephone Museum
12 Hancock Avenue
The Jefferson Barracks Telephone Museum is in an 1896 building that was originally a duplex for officers. It houses an extensive collection of telephones, telephone-related equipment and memorabilia dating from the 1880s to the 2000s, including military telephones used in World War I through the Gulf Wars and a replica of Alexander Graham Bell's 1877 First Commercial Telephone.

St. Louis Arsenal

Second and Arsenal Streets
St. Louis, MO 63118

The St. Louis Arsenal was established on this thirty-seven-acre site in 1827 to replace the arsenal at Fort Belle Fontaine. It has twenty-five buildings on the campus surrounded by a ten-foot stone wall. The arsenal played an important role in the Mexican-American War. It employed 517 workers to produce 19,500 artillery rounds, 8.4 million small arms cartridges, 13.7 million musket balls, 4.7 million rifle balls, 17 cannons, 15,700 small arms and 4,600 edged weapons.

It played a similar role in the Civil War and was the center of concern that led to the Camp Jackson Affair in May 1861.

After the Civil War, the arsenal became a military depot. Today, it remains an active military post, housing an installation of the National Geospatial-Intelligence Agency (NGA). The NGA collects, analyzes and distributes geospatial intelligence, including the making of maps for the U.S. military. It played an important role in locating the compound of Osama bin Laden for the raid that killed him. The NGA will be moving to a new campus in North St. Louis.

Lyon Park

3259 South Broadway
St. Louis, MO 63118

The ground for Lyon Park was given to the City of St. Louis by the federal government in 1869. An obelisk with Nathaniel Lyon's portrait on the front of a bronze plaque and a mythological creature holding symbols of war and peace on the back was erected in 1874. A statue of General Lyon was placed on the site of Camp Jackson in 1929 at Grand and Pine Streets. It was not well received. Critics said Lyon looked sick and about to fall off his horse. Moreover, his first name was misspelled. In 1960, Harriet Frost Fordyce, a wealthy philanthropist and youngest daughter of Daniel Frost, commander of the militia captured by Lyon in the Camp Jackson Affair, agreed to donate $1 million to expand the university on condition that the statue be removed. The city quickly agreed to move the statue to Lyon Park, where it remains today.

Soulard Market

730 Carroll Street
St. Louis, MO 63104

Antoine Soulard was a French army officer who fled his country to avoid the guillotine. He arrived in St. Louis in 1794 and established a fruit farm in what is today Lafayette Park. In 1795, Soulard married Julia Cerre, the daughter of Gabriel Cerre, one of the first European settlers in the city. Soulard established an open-air market at its present location in 1779. The property was, however, caught up in the litigation that arose after the Louisiana Purchase regarding Spanish land grants and was not settled until 1836, eleven years after Antoine's death. Julia donated two blocks to the City of St. Louis on condition that it remain a farmers market.

A tornado in 1896 destroyed the original building. It was replaced in 1929 by the current structure, a Renaissance-style building modeled after the Foundling Hospital designed by Filippo Brunelleschi in 1419 in Florence, Italy. The Grand Hall is shaped like the letter *H*, with vendor stalls in the four wings and a theater on the second floor. The market is open Wednesday through Saturday, offering fresh produce, meat, seafood, cheese, snacks, baked goods, spices, flowers and other merchandise.

The surrounding Soulard neighborhood has several historic buildings, including: the Trinity Lutheran Church and School at 812 Soulard Street, founded by German immigrants in 1839; the Saint Peter and Paul Church and School at Allen and Eighth Streets, built in 1875 to replace temporary buildings dating to 1849; and the Henry Soulard home at 1827 South Ninth Street, built in 1850 and featuring "6 over 6" windows. (The term refers to the number of glass panes on both the upper and lower portions of the window.)

Mary Meacham Freedom Crossing

4500 East Prairie Avenue
St. Louis, MO 63106

Mary Meacham was the wife of Reverend John Berry Meacham. John purchased his freedom and later that of Mary. He established the First African Baptist Church, the first Black congregation in St. Louis. John and Mary were active in the Underground Railroad, helping slaves escape to the Free State of Illinois. At this location on May 21, 1855, Mary was arrested by law enforcement officials for attempting to help five slaves cross the Mississippi River to freedom. She was tried and acquitted. During the Civil War, Mary was president of the Colored Ladies Soldiers' Aid Society in St. Louis. She died in 1869.

Each year, there is a celebration of Meacham's heroism at the crossing. It is located on the Mississippi Greenway, part of the Great Rivers Greenway, about three miles north of downtown. The site is included in the National Park Service's Underground Railroad to Freedom.

Old Courthouse

11 North Fourth Street
St. Louis, MO 63102

The Old Courthouse, as it is known today, is most famous as the site of the Dred Scott trials resulting in the Supreme Court opinion that fueled the flames that led to the Civil War. The land on which it sits was donated by August Chouteau and John B.C. Lucas in 1816. The first courthouse on the site was a brick structure completed in 1828. The rapid expansion of the city made that building obsolete within a decade. It was replaced by the current building in 1839, which incorporated the original courthouse as an east wing (one of four) with a dome in the center. It had twelve courtrooms altogether. The Dred Scott trials were held in one of the courtrooms in the west wing. The building was remodeled in 1851, and the old east wing was demolished and replaced

In addition to the Dred Scott case, the Old Courthouse was also the site of an unsuccessful lawsuit by Virginia Minor in the early fight for women's suffrage. *National Park Service.*

with an entirely new east wing. Due to the extensive remodeling, the original dome, a Classical Revival style, was replaced. The new dome was of wrought and cast iron with a copper exterior in an Italian Renaissance style, similar to that added to the United States Capitol Building during the Civil War.

In the 1930s, the City of St. Louis moved its courts to the new Civil Courts Building, a few blocks west. That structure was based on the Mausoleum of Halicarnassus, with an Ionic colonnade and Egyptian Revival stepped pyramid in correct proportions. The Old Courthouse was used by an art school and a charitable institution that refurbished toys for children. The Chouteau and Lucas families sued unsuccessfully to have the property reverted back to them. It was transferred to the federal government in 1940.

The Old Courthouse is now part of the Gateway Arch National Park. In 2012, a statue of Dred and Harriet Scott was dedicated on the south lawn of the courthouse. In 2022, a Freedom Suits Memorial was placed in front of the Civil Courts Building to commemorate the nearly four hundred lawsuits filed by slaves who sought their freedom through the courts in the way the Scotts attempted to do.

Ulysses S. Grant National Historic Site (White Haven)
7400 Grant Road
St. Louis, MO 63123

When guests leave the Visitor's Center at the Ulysses S. Grant National Historic Site to see White Haven, the house where Grant and his wife, Julia, met and lived, their first question often is, "Why is the house green?" White Haven wasn't named after the color of the house but after the Maryland plantation where Julia Grant's father, Frederick F. Dent, grew up. It was painted Paris green in 1874 by the Grants. The estate, now owned by the federal government and operated by the National Park Service, has a history that began before Missouri was a state. It was built by William Lindsay Long sometime between 1812 and 1816. Frederick Dent, a wealthy St. Louis merchant, bought the 850-acre farm in 1818. Not long after, Dent moved his family and the enslaved persons he brought from Maryland there.

As originally built, White Haven had four rooms: a parlor and dining room downstairs and two bedrooms upstairs. It has a third-floor attic that was used for storage and possibly as quarters for enslaved persons. Dent added an office at the rear of the house in 1818 and a sitting room in 1830. In the hallway between the dining room and the sitting room is a door that Dent's slaves used to enter the house. (They were not permitted to use the front or back doors.) Grant had a kitchen added to the house in 1868. It has two porches, one upstairs and one downstairs. Dent's seven children slept in one bedroom. During the scorching and humid St. Louis summers, they used the upstairs porch, entered from the hallway at the head of the staircase, as a sleeping porch to escape the stifling bedroom. Julia remembered the porch as her "piazza."

In rehabilitating and restoring the house, the National Park Service found the door that was the enslaved person's entrance and the exterior wall of the house—a bright green—as it existed after the Grants' purchase. The park service determined that it was a Paris green, a popular color for Victorian homes in the nineteenth century. It was decided to paint the entire house that shade, as it was the color chosen by Ulysses and Julia Grant. The house is believed to have been a beige color in the 1850s, when the Grants lived there with the Dent family.

Behind the house is a stone building erected around 1840 that was used as a summer kitchen and probably a home for some of Dent's enslaved persons. The winter kitchen is in the basement under the sitting room. Two red buildings stand on the edge of a shallow creek behind the home. One is the icehouse, probably built around 1840, and the chicken house, probably built between 1850 and 1870. The earlier date may be the most likely, because Julia wrote about her love for her chickens, which of course were actually cared for—not by her, but by the enslaved persons living there. Ulysses, who loved horses and intended to return to White Haven to raise them after his presidential term, built a stable in 1871. It was originally located near the modern homes seen from White Haven's front porch. It was moved in 1961, and then again in 2007, to its present location. The stable serves as the site's museum and is well worth a visit.

Frederick Dent owned as many as thirty enslaved people, making him one of the largest slaveholders in Missouri. Although Missouri was a slave state, most of its slave owners owned fewer than five slaves, many only one or two, who worked alongside their owner. Some of the enslaved persons who worked in the house as cooks or servants may have lived in the attic or in the stone summer kitchen. The field hands lived across the creek behind the house in what is now a suburban subdivision. The fields where the slaves worked were north of the house—where the parking lot and pasture for Grant's Farm are located.

The Civil War brought Grant to his destiny: appointment as commander of all Union armies, and ultimately, his election as president of the United States. Ulysses and Julia purchased White Haven following the Civil War, intending to make it their home. Instead, they moved to New York City after his presidential term ended. The Grants last visited White Haven in 1883.

White Haven is not white but Paris green, the color selected by Ulysses S. and Julia Dent Grant when they owned it. It was named after Julia's family plantation in Maryland. *Author photo.*

In 1885, Grant—beset by financial difficulties—sold White Haven to satisfy debts he had incurred through unfortunate investments. The farm remained in private hands until 1986, when it was sold to St. Louis County. In 1989, the National Park Service bought the house, its outbuildings and ten acres of land. The home underwent extensive restoration and archaeological investigation. Today, it is one of the most visited historic sites in the St. Louis area.

Hardscrabble, the cabin built by Grant nearby, has its own unique history. When Ulysses and Julia returned to St. Louis after he retired from the army (before the Civil War), they lived at White Haven until her father gave them land a short distance away. The structure was never equal to the home Julia was used to living in, and they moved back to White Haven after three months. When the Grants moved out of Hardscrabble, Julia's father sold the farm on her behalf to Joseph White for $7,200. White defaulted on the sale, and Julia repossessed it. However, she then leased it back to White. White defaulted on the lease, and Julia sued. The dispute ended up in the Missouri Supreme Court. The court rejected White's defense that Julia had no legal right to sue because she was a woman, and she regained control of the property. In 1884, the Grants mortgaged the property to William Vanderbilt, a New York tycoon, for a loan of $150,000. Grant lost the money in 1885 after being swindled by his business partner. Grant conveyed the property to Vanderbilt. In 1888,

Hardscrabble housed the Grant family for a short time when they resided in St. Louis. It is the only structure built by hand by a U.S. president that still exists. *Missouri Historical Society*.

Luther Conn bought the farm. He sold the farm but retained the right to sell the Hardscrabble cabin separately.

Conn sold the cabin to Edwin and Justin Joy, two real estate developers. They disassembled the structure, numbering each log, and reassembled it in the Old Orchard area of Webster Groves. C.F. Blanke bought the cabin in 1903 and moved it to the building now known as the St. Louis Art Museum for display during the St. Louis World's Fair in 1904 as an advertisement for his company's coffee. In 1907, August Busch Sr. bought the cabin and moved it to Grant's Farm, where it can be seen today when touring the farm, as well as from Gravois Road. It is the only surviving structure built by a U.S. president. The Daughters of the American Revolution placed a monument in St. Paul's Cemetery on the original site of Hardscrabble.

Bellefontaine Cemetery
4945 West Florissant Avenue
St. Louis, MO 63115
A stroll through Bellefontaine Cemetery gives visitors a delicious taste of St. Louis history. Many of the city's movers, shakers, scalawags and suffragettes, as a popular book by Carol Ferring Shepley on the history of the cemetery describes its inhabitants, are buried there. Going next door to the Archdiocesan Calvary Cemetery only adds to the picture.

In the early 1800s, burial practices across the nation changed. Before that, the departed found a home in churchyards and family cemeteries. As land was claimed for cities and development, the bodies—and where they were buried—moved away from city centers. Peaceful settings on the outskirts of cities were chosen for the specific purpose of burials. Because of the city's growth, a group of St. Louisans established a "rural" cemetery in 1849. There were twenty-two cemeteries in the city limits, and each was approaching capacity. Bodies were often buried, then dug up and reburied again and again as St. Louis claimed more and more space. Sadly, many of the burial places were poorly maintained and seemingly forgotten in the hustle and bustle of busy city life.

From its beginnings, Bellefontaine Cemetery was developed as an inspirational, cultural and educational institution. Founders wanted the cemetery to equal those in major eastern cities, whose ranks it wanted to join. Plans included being an architectural and horticultural showcase. The cemetery was an example of inclusivity from the start, welcoming those of all religions, races and social classes, as well as immigrants.

The 1849 cholera epidemic underscored the need for additional burial space. The trustees purchased 138 acres north of the city limits, including an existing family graveyard dating to 1817. The cemetery was dedicated on May 15, 1850. Today, the cemetery totals 314 acres and is less than half full, projecting the availability of burial spots for the next two hundred years. It is the oldest garden cemetery west of the Mississippi River and is also a Level 2 Arboretum. Due to a continuous tree-planting program, the cemetery today has nine thousand trees in five thousand varieties. Some trees are over a century old. There are native Missouri species, of course, but also some from around the world.

By the turn of the century, over one thousand people were buried each year. Family tombs lined Prospect Avenue, many architecturally significant. For example, Louis Sullivan designed not only the Wainwright Building in downtown St. Louis but also the Wainwright tomb. Today, Bellefontaine Cemetery has over eighty-seven thousand graves and includes many noteworthy individuals who contributed to the growth and development of St. Louis.

There are guided tours available throughout the year, often themed, such as steamboat captains or beer barons. Self-guided tours are offered at any time.

Among the prominent citizens interred in the cemetery are the following:

David R. Francis's most stellar achievement was serving as president of the Louisiana Purchase Exposition. He also was a successful businessman and politician. When he was mayor of St. Louis, he ran it like a business, and two of his important achievements were paving the streets and improving the water supply, both contributing to St. Louis being chosen as the site of the Louisiana Purchase Exposition. Serving as governor of Missouri, he cut spending and taxes and instituted via the legislature a secret ballot system of voting that led to fairer elections. He also created the nonpartisan curator system to govern the University of Missouri. In 1892, when fire destroyed the campus, he rebuilt it. As a result, the Quadrangle is named for him. His less successful venture was as ambassador to Russia during the Russian Revolution of 1917.

Sara Teasdale was a renowned poet and the recipient of the first Pulitzer Prize for poetry.

John Berry Meacham was born enslaved and bought his freedom. He was the founder of the First African American Baptist church in St. Louis. But even more important, he created the idea of Freedom Schools located on boats in the middle of the Mississippi River when Missouri made it illegal to teach African Americans to read and write.

One of the leaders of the Lewis and Clark expedition, William Clark, is buried in the cemetery. He returned to St. Louis and became territorial governor. Although he started as an Indian fighter, after the expedition, Clark realized that the group could never have made it without the assistance of Native Americans. He served as Indian superintendent in his later years. He is buried at the highest point of the cemetery, overlooking a point close to where the Mississippi River and Missouri River join. His grave, a simple obelisk with a bronze image of Clark, is one of the most visited sites in the cemetery.

Thomas Hart Benton—the politician, not the muralist—was the first U.S. senator from Missouri. He was known for his duel with Charles Lucas on Bloody Island, which resulted in his opponent's loss of life, an act Benton regretted until the end of his days.

Virginia Minor was a national leader of suffragists in the nineteenth century. After the Civil War, she sued for women's right to vote, unsuccessfully claiming that the Fourteenth Amendment gave them the right to vote as an incident of citizenship.

Adolphus Busch, the cofounder of Anheuser-Busch, is buried in a family mausoleum that cost $250,000 at the time of its construction. (It would cost $7.5 million to replace today.) His estate was the largest to be probated in the state of Missouri at the time of his death. It required twenty-five trucks to carry all the floral displays sent to the cemetery. A 250-piece band led the "parade," twenty miles long, to the cemetery. Busch was the first to pasteurize beer, meaning it would last longer without spoiling and could be shipped farther. He was also a proponent of vertical integration, meaning he brought all

The Busch Mausoleum was built at the death of August Busch Sr. The vine on the gates is reminiscent of Busch's favorite beverage, wine. *Author photo.*

the components it took to make his product together in his company, including bottling, ice plants, railroads and more.

James B. Eads was a man of many talents. He held more than fifty patents. He made his first fortune salvaging wrecked steamboats and their cargo with a diving bell he invented. He built ironclads for the Union navy during the Civil

War. Eads is most famous for designing the bridge spanning the Mississippi bearing his name, completed in 1874. It still carries automobile and light rail traffic today. The Eads Bridge was named a National Historic Landmark by the Department of the Interior and in October 1974 was listed as a National Historic Civil Engineering Landmark by the American Society of Civil Engineers.

William Greenleaf Eliot, a Unitarian minister who had a big impact on education in St. Louis, rests in the cemetery. He founded Washington University and Mary Institute (a private girls academy now merged with Country Day School) and served as president of the St. Louis School Board, bringing the district's schools much honor.

Have a copy of *The Joy of Cooking* on your kitchen shelf? The author of one of the most famous cookbooks in history, Irma Starkloff Rombauer, is buried in the cemetery.

Several members of the ill-fated Lemp family are buried in the largest mausoleum on the grounds. William Sr. commissioned the $60,000 tomb when his favorite son, Fred, died young.

Another suffragist, Edna Fischel Gellhorn, was a creator of the famous Golden Lane during the 1916 Democratic convention, held in St. Louis. To protest women's lack of the right to vote, seven thousand women lined the route by which delegates walked to the convention center. The women dressed in white with yellow sashes and carried yellow parasols.

Robert Campbell, the successful fur trader, entrepreneur and businessman who lived in Campbell House, also is interred in Bellefontaine Cemetery. Campbell negotiated treaties with the Plains Indians and raised, equipped and drilled four Missouri regiments for the Mexican-American War.

Two men famous in steamboat lore are buried in the cemetery. Samuel Gaty was a manufacturer of steamboat machinery. Captain William Massie carried the bullet that killed Wild Bill Hickok in his wrist until his death. That bullet also rests in the cemetery.

Of all graves in the cemetery, 15 percent are unmarked. On the scalawag scale, Eliza Haycraft ran a very successful house of ill-repute in the city but used her vast earnings to help others. She is buried in one of the unmarked graves. Cemetery trustees required this when she expressed her desire to be buried in the cemetery. She rests alone, under a sweet gum tree, in a very large, unmarked plot. Wealthy African Americans often chose not to have a marker, because it brought attention to the fact that their family had money.

One of the missions of the cemetery is to keep alive the stories of those buried on its grounds. And there are as many stories as there are graves, although not all are known. Kate Brewington Bennett's grave sports a large

Above: James Eads, builder of the Eads Bridge, is one of the many people important in St. Louis history buried in Bellefontaine Cemetery. *Author photo*.

Right: Hotchkiss Chapel has been recently refurbished. It has a chapel space as well as a columbarium. The chapel is named after the first two superintendents of the cemetery. *Author photo*.

marker with a statue of a reclining woman. Bennett is reputed to have been a beauty and said to have died for it. During her time, a pale face was a desired beauty trait, and she achieved her paleness using arsenic. Although not fatal in small doses, its effects build over time, and she ultimately succumbed to the substance. Another woman, Oma Vaughan, had her leg amputated and wanted to be reunited with it after her death. The leg was buried, before the woman, in Bellefontaine Cemetery. Unfortunately, when Vaughan died, she was buried elsewhere. Samuel Gaty has a period after his name on the obelisk marking his grave. This indicates that he had no sons to carry on the paternal name.

Calvary Cemetery
5239 West Florissant Avenue
St. Louis MO 63115

Calvary Cemetery was founded in 1854 by the Archdiocese of St. Louis, for many of the same reasons the Bellefontaine Cemetery was created, and because no more cemeteries were allowed within the city limits of St. Louis after the 1849 cholera epidemic, based on the mistaken belief that the graves of those who died of the disease could spread it. Archbishop Peter Richard Kenrick authorized the purchase of Old Orchard Farm, turning half of it into a cemetery and using the other half as his home. The cemetery is 470 acres and has three hundred thousand graves. About 20 percent of those interred are religious, priests and nuns. For example, Mary Odilia Berger founded the Franciscan Sisters of Mercy who run hospitals.

Other people of interest buried in Calvary include Mickey Carroll, a Munchkin in the *Wizard of Oz*. Kate Chopin, author of *The Awakening* and an acknowledged early feminist author, was born and then buried in St. Louis, although she lived a portion of her life in Louisiana. Auguste Chouteau, the cofounder of St. Louis, was first buried in the original village of St. Louis and later reinterred in Calvary along with his mother, Marie Chouteau, the first white woman to live in St. Louis and often acknowledged as the mother of the city. The first governor of Missouri, Alexander McNair, rests in the cemetery, as does Dred Scott, whose suit for freedom is a landmark case. His wife, Harriet, who was also part of the legal action, is buried in Greenwood Cemetery, the first commercial, nonsectarian African American cemetery in St. Louis. William Tecumseh Sherman, the Union general known for his "March to the Sea" during the Civil War, is interred at Calvary. And the Pulitzer Prize–winning playwright Tennessee Williams chose St. Louis' Calvary Cemetery as his final resting place. The land purchased for the cemetery from Senator Henry Clay had existing graves for soldiers from Fort Bellefontaine and some Native Americans. Those graves were dug up and the people reburied in a mass grave marked by a crucifix.

The Campbell House Museum

1508 Locust St.,
St. Louis, MO 63103

From the front, the Campbell House looks like a row house, but it has always been freestanding. At the time, it was both unusual and expensive to build houses on separate lots. The home was the first house completed on Lucas Place, in 1851. While the family lived there, it became the center of St. Louis society. Lucas Place was the first private residential street in St. Louis. It was built on farmland and a part of St. Louis's original Common Fields, traditional French communal farms dating to the earliest years of the city. The street was the first in the city to require houses to be set back from the street. There were also deed restrictions prohibiting theaters, dram shops and coffee shops from locating on Lucas Place. The house itself was a three-story, Victorian townhouse with both attic and basement as well as the luxury of running water. The Campbells purchased the practically new home in 1854 for $13,600.

Robert Campbell was born in Ireland, a second son with no prospects. He craved adventure and traveled to the United States in 1822. Campbell had no education to speak of, but he was an astute businessman. From 1824 to 1835, he worked as a fur trader. John O'Fallon hired him as a clerk in his fur-trading business, but Campbell soon headed west, partly for his health and partly for the adventure. After learning the ins and outs of fur trading, he joined forces with William Sublette in their own company. When he wasn't on business in the western mountains, Campbell returned to St. Louis. The partners had the foresight to see the coming end to the fur trade boom and set up a dry-goods business in the city. Their timing was perfect, as people used St. Louis as staging point to acquire supplies for their move west and the population of the city tripled. After an economic downturn in 1842, Sublette left the dry-goods business, but Campbell continued. He expanded his business empire, becoming one of the richest men in the country by including in his portfolio real estate, banking and transportation. He owned steamboats, invested in trains and the Southern Hotel (one of the premier hotels in St. Louis in the mid-nineteenth century) and provisioned the Union army in Missouri during the Civil War.

In 1835, Campbell spent time with his brother in Philadelphia, recovering from a bout of mountain fever. His sister-in-law's cousin, the thirteen-year-old Virginia Kyle, helped nurse the thirty-one-year-old Campbell back to health and in the process became fascinated with him and his stories. Although everyone he knew objected, Campbell proposed to Virginia three years later. Her mother would not allow her daughter to marry. Campbell waited three more years, and the two wed in 1841. The couple made their home in St. Louis, where Virginia set out to be a fashionable hostess.

All the riches the Campbell family accumulated did not protect them from loss. For example, the year 1849 was a bad one for St. Louis in general. There was a tragic fire that wiped out much of downtown, including Campbell's general store, and a cholera epidemic took 10 percent of the city's population. The oldest child of Robert and Virginia died at the age of seven during the epidemic.

The Campbells lost ten of their thirteen children before they reached the age of eight. Only three sons, Hugh, Hazlett and James (each bearing the recycled name of an earlier, deceased sibling), survived to adulthood. None married and all lived off the family fortune. James, the youngest of the three, attended Yale and Harvard. He and Hugh traveled abroad several times. While the two of them were living in Paris, James died.

Hugh, the oldest survivor, returned to St. Louis after that to take care of Hazlett, who suffered from mental illness, and to manage his father's businesses. The men continued to live in the home on Lucas Place. One of Hugh's projects was taking care of newsboys in the city by supporting Father Dunne's Newsboys Home. Hazlett, perhaps as a result of lead poisoning from the running water in the home, was afflicted with either schizophrenia or manic depression. After Hugh died, Hazlett was taken care of under provisions of the will. He died in 1938, having lived his entire life in the Campbell House. At that time, the house passed to Yale University under the terms of Hugh's will.

From the front, the Campbell House looks like a row house, but it was always a single-family home. *St. Louis Landmarks.*

Some of the famous people to visit the family included William Clark, Jim Bridger, Karl Bodner (artist known for his western landscapes), Kit Carson, Washington Irving, Mark Twain, William Tecumseh Sherman and Ulysses S Grant.

It's no wonder that preservationists wanted to save the home. It was the last surviving home on Lucas Place, the last chance to save a portion of history so important to St. Louis and the story of westward expansion. Several organizations banded together and raised $6,000 to purchase some of the family's belongings at an auction held in 1941. Other items were donated by purchasers. In 1942, Yale sold the house to the Campbell House Foundation, helped by a generous grant from the department store Stix, Baer and Fuller. The museum opened in 1943, with many of the original furnishings placed exactly the way the Campbell family had them. This was possible due to a series of photos taken about 1885 that survive to this day. The photos offer a unique look into the world at that time and are available to view online.

Chatillon-DeMenil House
3352 DeMenil Place
St. Louis, MO 63118

Frances Parkman was a twenty-two-year-old academic who wanted firsthand knowledge of how the Native Americans of the Plains lived for a planned historical work on the French and Indian War. Friends in St. Louis introduced him to Henri Chatillon as a possible guide. When they returned from their journey to the Rockies, Parkman spent the next year in bed, recovering from an illness and writing *The Oregon Trail: Sketches of Prairie and Rocky-Mountain Life*. The book became a classic of American history and a guide for many on their way west, but it also immortalized the original owner of the Chatillon-DeMenil House.

Chatillon was the grandson of Clement de Treger, the founder of Carondelet, a town separate from St. Louis at the time. He was a trapper and mountain man and worked for the American Fur Company. Chatillon married a Sioux woman named Bear Robe, the daughter of a powerful chief. While serving as Parkman's guide, Chatillon received word that his wife was ill. Henri and Parkman's cousin Quincy Shaw, who was traveling with them, detoured to the village where Bear Robe lay dying. Henri and Quincy reached her, as Parkman later wrote, "just in time to hear the death rattle in her throat." Henri returned to the Parkman expedition in deep mourning.

Chatillon's loss of his first wife may be the source of a mysterious painting found in the attic when the house underwent renovations in the 1960s. The painting depicts a handsome, sad-eyed man and a Native American woman in two profile views. The people are believed to be Chatillon and Bear Robe. It was wrapped in leather around a Hawken rifle that had been the gift of Parkman. Bear Robe and Parkman had an indelible effect on the life of Henri Chatillon.

Henri returned to St. Louis and, in 1848, married Odile Delor Lux, his cousin and a wealthy woman. She owned twenty-one acres of land that became the site of the original four-room, brick farmhouse that forms the heart of the Chatillon-DeMenil House. They lived in the house until he sold it to Dr. Nicolas DeMenil and his partner Eugene Mittenberger in 1856. The Chatillons returned to Carondelet. The marriage to Odile was childless, but Chatillon's older daughter with Bear Robe came to St. Louis in 1858, was baptized and married in the Catholic church to a trader she met in what would later become Wyoming. She and her husband had three children.

Dr. DeMenil came to St. Louis in 1834 and practiced medicine on Chouteau's Row. He married Emilie Sophie Chouteau, a descendant of St. Louis' founders. In 1861, he renovated the four-room farmhouse he'd bought into a mansion, completing the work in 1864. By then, he had retired from the practice of medicine and was involved in land speculation, a business that made him a wealthy man. He was also reputedly the co-owner of St. Louis' first drugstore chain.

Emilie Sophie and Nicolas had one son, Alexander, who lived in the home until he died in 1928. He was on the board of directors of the 1904 World's Fair and served as a translator to French dignitaries to the fair. He amassed a collection of World's Fair memorabilia displayed in the top floor of the house. Alexander was a scholar and published a journal of literary criticism, *The Hesperian*. He also served on many boards, such as the Missouri Historical Society, and made contributions to St. Louis and Missouri history. However, he was a critic of ragtime culture, Mark Twain and Walt Whitman.

After Alexander no longer lived in the home, caretakers were in charge until 1945, when it was purchased by Lee Hess, who turned the caves under the property into a tourist attraction. The natural limestone caves were used by brewers as early as the 1840s. The portion under the Chatillon-DeMenil House may have been used by Minnehaha Beer Company, which ceased production in 1867. There was no entrance to the caves from the Chatillon-DeMenil home.

Lemp Brewery used most of the caves for storage and lagering, the process of maturation of beer at near freezing temperatures. Eventually, William Lemp

The Chatillons built this home as a four-room farmhouse. The DeMenils turned it into the mansion pictured here. *Author photo.*

built his large brewing plant over the caves. The Lemp sections of the caves separated the lagering rooms with masonry walls, had arched doorways and used brick-lined trenches to drain excess water. Ice holes were created for workers to drop ice into the caves to keep a proper temperature. After refrigeration came into play, the Lemp family used the caves for entertainment, creating a theater and a swimming pool.

While Hess was cleaning the caves, he found the bones of a prehistoric pig. The curator of the American Museum of Natural History came to St. Louis and catalogued over three thousand fossils in the caves. Hess touted the natural beauty of the caves to visitors and created exhibits. He bought the Damascus Palace from the Chicago World's Fair and the 1904 World's Fair and displayed them in the caves. The caves were open for tourists until 1960. During the construction of Interstate 55, the entrance imploded, and the caves are no longer accessible.

While Hess owned the property, the house was deserted and much of the interior decor was stolen.

The house was in danger of being demolished when Interstate 55 was planned, but Union Electric stepped in with a donation, making it possible for the Landmarks Association to buy the home and restore it.

Today, the home operates as a museum featuring nineteenth- and twentieth-century furnishings and decorative arts belonging to the DeMenil family and other important St. Louis families. The furniture in Emilie Sophie's bedroom is original to the family and home.

Eugene Field House

634 South Broadway
St. Louis, MO 63102

The Eugene Field House, constructed in 1845, was originally one of twelve attached row houses known as Walsh's Row. Eleven of the connected homes were demolished in 1936, leaving only the Field House to become the first historic house museum to open in St. Louis (December 18, 1936). The home commemorates the "children's poet," as Eugene Field came to be known. Field was born in St. Louis in 1850 and claimed two birth dates, September 2 and 3, so if friends forgot to wish him a happy birthday on one, they could send their wish on the other. He spent only a few years in the St. Louis home. He was sent to live with an aunt in Massachusetts after his mother died when he was six years old.

Children's poet Eugene Field spent his early years in this row house in St. Louis. His father, Roswell Field, was involved in the Dred Scott case that brought the nation one step closer to civil war. *St. Louis Landmarks.*

Eugene's father, Roswell, had his own measure of fame. He represented Dred and Harriet Scott in their freedom case, an important decision that helped pave the way to the Civil War.

After studying at the University of Missouri, Field became a journalist at various newspapers throughout the Midwest, including stints in St. Louis. Along the way, he wrote children's poems, such as "Wynken, Blynken and Nod," that were part of many schoolchildren's memories, as they were required to memorize them, especially in the grade schools across the state named after him.

The home features original furnishings from the Field family, as well as a toy collection and a library. The library is a collection of Eugene Field works, including first-edition books and manuscripts. Research opportunities are available by appointment.

St. Francis Xavier College Church

3628 Lindell Boulevard
St. Louis, MO 63108

Even before the recent pandemic, St. Louis suffered through epidemics of other diseases. How did citizens deal with them at the time? Interestingly, many relied on prayer, with what seems like miraculous results.

The year 1849 was not a good one for St. Louis. In addition to a great fire that destroyed much of the riverfront and downtown, the city also was hit with a cholera epidemic. People started falling ill in January, perhaps due to the disease being carried into the city by a steamboat, and deaths peaked from late April to mid-July. During that time, officials screened new arrivals to the city. If they showed symptoms of disease, they were sent to Quarantine Island. As many as seven thousand to eight thousand people in the city of seventy-seven thousand died. Some days saw as many as two hundred funerals.

At that time, Saint Louis University, a descendant of the St. Louis Academy and founded by the Jesuits, was all male. Enrollment listed two hundred boarders plus additional day students from the area. Prayer services were held every day at St. Francis Xavier Church, and the Sodality of the Blessed Virgin Mary added extra daily prayers. The group gathered in the Our Lady Chapel in front of the statue that still stands outside the chapel to ask Mary's protection for the student body against cholera. The men promised that if none of them living at the university died from the disease, they would place a silver crown on the statue as a memorial of her love. The students also placed medals of the Immaculate Conception on the gate and doors. Students lost a lot of their fear of the disease, believing that the Blessed Mother would protect them

The university dismissed classes in June, and the men returned to their homes. When the danger passed in the fall, the students returned. None of the students contracted cholera, nor did any of the Jesuits who had spent most of their time during the epidemic caring for the sick. On October 8, the group gathered to fulfill its promise and crown the statue. (The students were of course wealthy, young and healthy and had access to better water than most of the city's population.)

The statue in question, carved from white stone and smaller than life size, stands today across from a small chapel in the basement of St. Francis Xavier Church. The crown spends its time either in the church or St. Louis University's museum. The marble plaque created by the Sodality of the Blessed Virgin Mary is also in storage, replaced by a bronze plaque that tells the story. The statue, crown and marble plaque are among the few artifacts that still exist from the early days of the church.

The Shrine of St. Joseph
1220 North Ninth Street
St. Louis, MO 63106

The cholera epidemic of 1849 wasn't the only time the disease struck St. Louis. Another epidemic in 1866 hit the German immigrant parish of St. Joseph on the north side of downtown with a vengeance. The pastor, Father Joseph Weber, and the parishioners vowed that if God protected them from the epidemic, they would erect a monument to St. Joseph in thanksgiving. They backed the vow with monetary donations of $4,000 ($82,600 in today's terms). Not one person in any family that signed the vow and pledge died of cholera.

The parish built a splendid altar, a replica of the Altar of St. Ignatius in the Church of the Gesu, the mother church of the Jesuits in Rome. The difference is that St. Ignatius is, of course, replaced by St. Joseph and the Christ Child. The altar is known as the Altar of Answered Prayers.

The Shrine of St. Joseph, founded by the Jesuits in 1843, is also the site of the only Vatican-authenticated miracle in a midwestern church. In 1864, a German immigrant, Ignatius Strecker, received an injury to his chest while at work. After several years of treatment, he was told the injury was fatal and to prepare for death. Father Francis Xavier Weninger happened to visit St. Joseph's while Strecker lay dying. His message was about Blessed Peter Claver, who was believed to be close to God. Mrs. Strecker was moved by Weninger's words and convinced her dying husband to visit the church and ask Blessed Peter Claver to intercede for him. Strecker dragged himself to the church, and Father Weninger blessed him with and allowed him to kiss a relic of Claver. Strecker's wound healed, he returned to work and completely recovered. The Vatican verified this as one of two miracles needed for the canonization of Blessed Peter Claver, who was declared a saint in 1888.

The shrine is open to the public, and Mass is celebrated on Sunday.

Mercantile Library
Thomas Jefferson Library Building
University of Missouri–St. Louis
1 University Boulevard
St. Louis, MO 63121

The St. Louis Mercantile Library is the oldest general library in continuous existence west of the Mississippi River. Even when St. Louis was a rough and tumble frontier town, city leaders felt it important that citizens have access to a library. The library is now, as it was from the beginning, a subscriber library. There were at one time one thousand mercantile libraries. Today, there are only ten.

In 1846, when the library was founded by James Yeatman, it was located in a warehouse near where the south leg of the Gateway Arch is located today. In 1854, it moved to a building located on the southwest corner of Broadway. The library provided one of the best and most historic meeting halls in the state. The convention called to consider secession met there in 1861—voting eighty-nine to one to remain in the Union. In January 1865, delegates met to approve a new state constitution that not only provided for the first time a system of free, public education in Missouri but also abolished slavery in the state.

The Mercantile Library spent its longest tenure so far in the building it moved to in 1889 at 510 Locust Street. The building survives, but in 1997 the library, due to expenses, merged with the University of Missouri–St. Louis and moved to its campus.

The early library was home away from home for many St. Louis leaders. Some would meet to play chess, including Joseph Pulitzer. The Mercantile Library was also the first art museum in St. Louis. Although many of its treasures have been donated to the St. Louis Art Museum, the library still boasts a collection of early nineteenth and twentieth-century regional artists, including George Caleb Bingham, Thomas Hart Benton, Charles Deas, Harriet Hosmer and more. William Tecumseh Sherman, a member of the Mercantile, donated a collection of George Catlin paintings

The core collection of 250,000 books centers on westward expansion, railroad and river transportation and the history, development and growth of St. Louis. There are collections within the main collection such as the John W. Barriger III National Railroad Library and the Herman T. Pott National Inland Waterways Library.

The library, among other artifacts and items, holds newspaper archives (including the St. Louis Globe-Democrat), presidential letters, early travel diaries, Civil War–era letters and records of the fur trade.

The fifteen thousand volumes from Herman T. Pott covering the history of American inland rivers and waterways form the core of the Herman T. Pott National Inland Waterways Library. Pott (1895–1982) was a river transportation executive who built boats and barges in Carondelet. During World War II, his company, St. Louis Shipbuilding and Steel, constructed ships for the United States and Russia. After purchasing Federal Barge Lines in 1953, the company became the world's largest designer and builder of inland river towboats.

Herman Pott, the son of German immigrants, was born in Wisconsin in 1895. He graduated with a degree in civil engineering from the University of Wisconsin in 1916 and went on to put his degree to use in innovating river transportation. One of his early improvements was welding the hulls of ships rather than using rivets. He also was an early proponent of diesel propulsion. Pott married Phenie Hope Ryals, a longtime St. Louis volunteer and philanthropist. The Salvation Army, Missouri Girls Town and the Missouri Botanical Garden were recipients of her time and treasure. Today, the Pott name lives on, not only in the library but also in the Pott Foundation. The foundation awards grants, mostly in the St. Louis area, to organizations that honor the values important to the Potts: education, children and health and human services.

The Mercantile Library also includes the personal library of Ruth Ferris, a well-known historian and writer on the topic of U.S. inland waterways. It also includes a donation from the *Waterways Journal*, including books on navigation and the economics of rivers.

John Walker Barriger (1899–1976) was a railroad executive and lifelong scholar of the railroad industry and its history. Over time, he collected books and corporate papers and took thousands of photos that form the heart of the John W. Barriger III National Railroad Library. He began his railroad career at the Pennsylvania Railroad in the 1920s. He served in Franklin D. Roosevelt's administration as chief of the Railroad Division of the Reconstruction Finance Corporation during the Depression. During World War II, he worked in the Office of Defense Transportation, then went on to become president of Monon Railroad, Pittsburgh and Lake Erie Railroad, and the Missouri-Kansas-Texas ("Katy") Railroad, as well as the Boston and Maine Railroad.

Barriger collected over fifteen thousand books covering all aspects of railroads from the 1820s and through his lifetime. Another thirty thousand volumes were books, pamphlets and industrial reports, donated by the Association of American Railroads–Bureau of Railroad Economic History in 1995. In addition, the library contains the Isabel H. Benham Papers, research files that include reports and analyses of traffic, finances and railroad operations; the ACF (American Car & Foundry Company) Industries Collection of corporate archives and photos of many of the cars built by the company; the GM&O Historical Society Collection, which includes maps, documents, reports, time tables and photos of the trains and people of this company; the Milwaukee Road Archives; and the Charles Rupp Railroad Time Table Collection.

One of the interesting aspects of the Barriger Collection is the fifty thousand photos he took himself. He was never without his camera and had a unique way of making decisions, starting mostly when he worked for the Reconstruction Finance Corporation during the Depression. In this job, he was responsible for deciding whether railroads applying for loans qualified. He used his photos of railroad infrastructure to pinpoint what was wrong. This method was successful enough in curing the ills that beset trains that he became known as the "doctor of sick railroads." He didn't take pictures only of trains; he also photographed rails, equipment and every aspect of railroading. The photos are well organized, making the collection even more valuable. Two of the secretaries at the RFC were responsible for cataloging the photos Barriger took during his tenure there. But even after the secretaries returned to their home states and he moved on to working at various railroads, Barriger would bring them back to keep the albums up to date.

The collections at Mercantile Library are available for browsing, research and interlibrary loan.

Chapter 5

ST. LOUIS AND BEER

Beer was king in the brewing mecca of St. Louis. Today, when we think of St. Louis beers, we think of Anheuser-Busch, but in its more than two hundred years, the city has been the home of over one hundred breweries. Even in the earliest days of the city, small breweries distributed beer locally. With the influx of German immigrants in the 1840s, beer and breweries came into their own. By 1860, there were forty breweries in St. Louis producing two hundred thousand barrels of beer a year.

Adam Lemp came to St. Louis from Germany (with a possible stop in Cincinnati) about 1838, working first as a grocer. But he continued to brew beer as he had in Germany. He opened a brewery a few years later, finding that the caves in St. Louis were perfect at providing the cooler temperatures needed to produce the lighter, golden lager popular in his homeland. This eventually became the norm. Lemp purchased a home on South Second Street (demolished to make way for the Gateway Arch) in 1840–41 to brew his product, and he grew his business from that location. The Lemp Brewery would eventually become one of the country's largest beer producers.

George Schneider created the Bavarian Brewery, the company that eventually became Anheuser-Busch, in 1852. Eberhard Anheuser originally produced soap and candles, not beer. After coming to St. Louis, he became a partner in the Bavarian Brewery, eventually becoming the principal owner and renaming it E. Anheuser & Company. Adolphus Busch started in a different aspect of the brewing business: supplies. He first met Anheuser through his work and then met Anheuser's daughter Lilly. They married, and Adolphus came to work at the brewery, eventually becoming his father-in-law's partner.

In the years following the Civil War, St. Louis became the third-largest beer producer in the nation. The Industrial Revolution meant big improvements in the beer brewing industry. Anheuser-Busch was the first to use pasteurization, making it possible to ship beer longer distances without fear of spoiling. Refrigeration advances eliminated the use of caves to provide cooling, The growth of railroads and the use of refrigerated railcars also meant that beer could be shipped all over the country. All of these things combined to turn local breweries like Lemp and Anheuser-Busch into national businesses. In fact, Anheuser-Busch grew to be the world's largest brewery. The popularity and growth of Anheuser-Busch beer was enhanced by Adolphus Busch's innovative marketing and promotion. For example, he pioneered the use of giveaways to promote the brand and turned the brewery into a tourist attraction by opening it for tours (still a tradition at the St. Louis brewery today).

Adolphus Busch, as a director of the 1904 World's Fair, joined all local breweries to create a six-acre biergarten at the fair called the Tyrolean Alps, a massive success.

This golden age of brewing ended with Prohibition in 1920. Breweries had to turn to other products, such as soft drinks and near beer, to survive the next thirteen years. However, in St. Louis, only eight of the twenty breweries that existed before Prohibition survived. The Lemp Brewery was the largest to close. By the 1950s, only two breweries were alive in St. Louis, Anheuser-Busch and Falstaff. Falstaff closed its plant in late 1977, and then there was one.

Today, local brews have made a comeback, and St. Louis has embraced the movement. Schlafly's St. Louis Brewery led the way for more craft breweries and brewpubs, usually connected to a restaurant.

In 2008, InBev took over Anheuser-Busch, making it the largest brewery in the world.

There are currently sixty-five breweries operating or planning to open in the St. Louis region.

The clock on the tower at the Anheuser-Busch Brewery is a St. Louis landmark and the second most photographed site in the city. *Author photo*.

Anheuser-Busch Brewery

610 Pestalozzi Street

St. Louis, MO 63118

The history of Anheuser-Busch is synonymous with the history of brewing in St. Louis. The brewery opened on Pestalozzi in the 1850s and opened for public tours in the 1890s, an idea birthed by Adolphus Busch.

The Clydesdales are always a highlight of the tour. August A. Busch gave his father the first team of Clydesdales in 1933 to celebrate the repeal of Prohibition.

The Brew House is six stories tall and was built in 1891. The hop vine chandeliers date to the 1904 World's Fair, and the clock tower is a local landmark. The Lyon School House served as the headquarters for the company from 1907 to 1981 and is the oldest building in the complex. It's the only place to see beechwood aging and fermentation cellars, as A-B is the only brewer to continue to use this process. The Bevo Packaging Plant dates to 1917. It is eight stories tall, covers twenty-seven acres and has twenty-five miles of conveyor belts on which bottles and cans are filled.

Lemp Mansion

3322 DeMenil Place

St. Louis, MO 63118

The life of the Lemp family is a definitive illustration that money can't buy happiness. Their home is the site of many tragic deaths and is reputed to be haunted by ghosts of the melancholy family.

The founder of America's Lemp family, John Adam Lemp, moved to St. Louis from Germany in 1838. He started his life in America as a grocer but sold lager beer as well. His father taught him beer brewing before he left home, and Lemp realized once in St. Louis that the caves under the city were perfect for aging beer. When he realized the potential of brewing, he left the grocery store and built the successful Western Brewery Company downtown (near where the Gateway Arch now stands). The first Lemp became a millionaire by giving the many Germans who had moved to St. Louis the beer they preferred, lager beer with a lighter taste and color than most served in the city.

Adam's son Wilhelm (later William) J. joined him in the city in 1848. William graduated from St. Louis University and went to work at the brewery. He joined the local infantry when the Civil War broke out as a supply officer and by war's end had reached the rank of lieutenant colonel. He married Julia Feickert in 1861. Her parents were the original owners of Lemp Mansion. William and

Julia and their family joined them in the mansion as the parents aged and the family grew.

After the death of Adam, his brewery passed equally to William and his cousin Charles Brauneck. William bought out his cousin's share and took over the business. In 1865, he built a new brewing plant at Cherokee and Carondolet that eventually covered five city blocks. By 1870, it not only was the largest brewery in St. Louis but also had the largest market share of the product. The brewery was connected to the mansion by a tunnel through the caves underneath the streets. William introduced artificial refrigeration, eliminating the need for the caves, and bottling beer in the brewery, making delivery of kegs to saloons obsolete. He also changed the name to William J. Lemp Brewing Company.

Annie, the oldest daughter, married, then, in a highly publicized proceeding, divorced her husband and married the man at the center of the marriage breakup. Annie became a New York City society matron and later an acclaimed writer, not of fiction but of French literature criticism and history.

In 1897, Lemp's daughter Hilda married Gustav Pabst of the Milwaukee brewing family. Pabst had been married and divorced. Lemp wanted to delay the wedding to his daughter until after a family vacation to Europe. However, Pabst didn't want to wait and followed Hilda and the Lemps to England, where the couple married in London. Gustav Pabst's brother also married an heiress to a beer dynasty, that of the Schlitz brewery, resulting in a three-way connection among major breweries.

The Lemp Brewery continued to grow and prosper. William was the first brewer to go national and ship beer in refrigerated railcars across the country. The best known of his beers today is Falstaff. He also created a pipeline that carried his product directly from the stock house to the bottling plant.

Frederick Lemp was the fourth son and his father's favorite. He was well known to be the son earmarked to take over the plant when William was gone, and he relished the role. Frederick was married and a new father when he began to suffer from ill health. He and his family relocated temporarily to California, and he improved, only to relapse and die from heart failure. William was devastated by the death. The trauma was doubled when his best friend, Frederick Pabst, also died.

On February 13, 1904, William Lemp locked the door to his bedroom and shot himself in the head. Only two years later, his wife, Julia, died of cancer.

Louis, the second son, left the brewery after the death of his mother. He loved horses, a love shared by other family members, as well as racing, and he had an interest in politics. He moved to New York and died in 1931 at the age of sixty-one.

William Lemp Jr., known as Billy, was the second child and oldest son of the dynasty. Billy became the reluctant head of the brewing company at his father's death. His interests ran more in the "playboy" vein, and he was an avid sportsman, although both pursuits were somewhat limited due to his responsibilities in the family business. After a scandal, he and his wife were divorced. He remarried several years later and became the first Lemp to move his residence away from the brewery headquarters. The Lemp Mansion was turned into offices. Prohibition was approaching, but Billy continued to fight, using all his creativity. He used an advertising postcard to commemorate Lemp Brewing transporting the first case of beer (Falstaff) via airplane from St. Louis to New Orleans. However, if the story is true, the pilot emptied the case of beer before reaching his destination. Billy was also the first to use trucks to deliver his product.

Then came January 16, 1920: Prohibition. Billy tried to pivot, producing a near beer called Cerva, but it wasn't selling well enough to cover the costs of keeping the brewery alive. Employees said that one day they showed up at the plant and the doors were locked, never to open for beer production again.

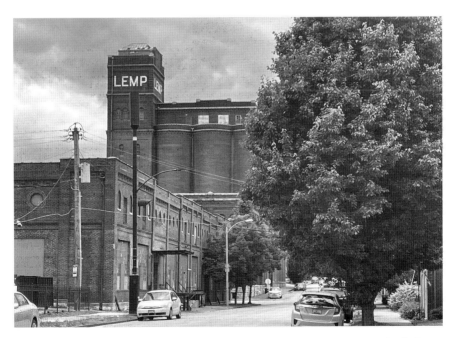

The Lemp Brewery hasn't been used as a brewery or been owned by the Lemp family in many years, but the name is still on the smokestack, marking an important time in St. Louis history. *Author photo.*

The Lemp Mansion, site of much tragedy, is now a restaurant and a bed-and-breakfast. Ghost tours are also available, if you dare. *Author photo.*

Also in 1920, the third daughter, Elsa, who at one time was the most sought-after heiress in St. Louis, committed suicide under mysterious circumstances. She had married, unhappily, and divorced, then remarried Thomas Wright. Elsa suffered from depression and soon after her remarriage was found in her bed in her home in the Central West End with a bullet wound to the chest.

Believing Prohibition would never end, Billy sold the Falstaff name to a fellow brewer (Griesedieck) and auctioned the brewery building, selling it to International Shoe Company for a paltry eight cents on the dollar. Billy, too, committed suicide, shooting himself in the heart in his office in the Lemp Mansion on December 29, 1922.

The fourth Lemp suicide also occurred at the mansion. Charles Lemp, after working at the brewery, went on to have a banking and political career. He was a reclusive bachelor and plagued by arthritis. In 1949, he shot himself in his bedroom.

William J. Lemp III, Billy's son, returned to St. Louis and tried to restart the Lemp Brewery, with no success. He dropped dead of a heart attack at age forty-three.

The final Lemp brother died in 1970 at age ninety.

The Lemp name is still visible on the smokestack tower of the old brewery on Cherokee Street. The Lemp Mansion operates today as a restaurant and bed-and-breakfast and features ghost tours, applicable no doubt to a house that has seen as much tragedy as the Lemp home has.

The mansion was built in the early 1860s and had thirty-three rooms. Radiator heat (still working) was installed in 1884 soon after it was patented. An elevator replaced the grand staircase, although all that is left of it today is the iron gate in the basement. The ceiling in the parlor was hand painted, and an atrium was built to house the Lemps' exotic birds and plants. The main bathroom on the first floor, used by William, features a glass-enclosed freestanding shower that William first saw in Italy and had shipped back to St. Louis. The bathroom also had a barber chair and a sink with glass legs. At the back of the house stand three vaults used to store the family's art collection, a collection so large it couldn't be displayed all at once. The second floor had bedrooms for the family, and the third floor was servants' quarters. The house also had a ballroom, auditorium and swimming pool in the "basement," a natural cave. The swimming pool was warmed by hot water from the nearby brewery. The kitchen and wine and beer cellars were also in the basement.

Grant's Farm

10501 Gravois Road
St. Louis, MO 63123

Grant's Farm is also a chapter in the story of the Busch family and beer in St. Louis. The farm, purchased from the Dent-Grant families, has been the Busch family home since 1903. The location was chosen because it was easy to access the breweries from there. Originally, the "farm" was a private park for the family, but it opened to the public in 1954 as an animal reserve. Buffalo, elephants, camels, kangaroos, donkeys, goats, peacocks and, of course, the world-famous Clydesdales, among other animals, roam the property.

In honor of the previous owner, August Busch Sr. bought President Ulysses S. Grant's home, Hardscrabble, and moved it to the property after the 1904 World's Fair. It is the only hand-built structure by a U.S. president still standing.

Covering 281 acres, Grant's Farm is a refuge for more than nine hundred animals. The centerpiece of the farm is the German-style stables and the Bauernhof, where food and beverages, including free beer, an Anheuser-Busch tradition, is offered.

As of November 2021, five members of the Busch family own and operate Grant's Farm.

Chapter 6

POST-CIVIL WAR ST. LOUIS

I n November 1864, Missouri held its first statewide election since the firing on Fort Sumter. Radicals won the governorship, the state legislature and a convention called to write a new constitution. The convention met at the Mercantile Library and on January 11, 1865, voted sixty to four to abolish slavery in Missouri (three weeks before Congress approved and sent to the states the Thirteenth Amendment abolishing slavery nationally). The new constitution instituted the Ironclad Oath, prohibiting anyone who had aided the rebellion in even the most trivial ways from holding public office, teaching and even the ministry. It was ruled unconstitutional by the U.S. Supreme Court a few years later.

The City of St. Louis expanded from 160,000 persons in 1860 to 204,000 in 1865. We don't know what its population was in 1870, because the census that year in the city was widely denounced as fraudulent. Instead of the 310,000 recorded in the census, it was likely about 230,000, more than half of whom were German or Irish immigrants or first-generation descendants.

The growing importance of railroads made it imperative that the Mississippi River be bridged. James B. Eads, who made his fortune before the Civil War salvaging sunken steamboats and who built ironclads during the war for the navy, designed a revolutionary double-decked arch bridge that would span the river. Excavation began in 1868, and the bridge was finally completed in 1874. Its construction was controversial. Because of the depth of the piers, workers experienced the "bends" and needed to decompress on return to the surface. Eads was aware of the dangers from

The Eads Bridge, a marvel of engineering, connects Missouri and Illinois. It is still in use today. *St. Louis Landmarks.*

his steamboat salvage business, yet 14 workers died and 114 suffered severe injuries. The Eads Bridge is still in use today, carrying both vehicular traffic and Metro rapid-transit trains.

The growing city also needed a better water supply, essential for expansion. It built a series of water towers and reservoirs to hold and supply water to residences and businesses. Three survive today in the city (of only seven in the entire nation): Compton Heights (now part of Compton Heights Reservoir Park), Water Tower #1 (also known as the White Tower and the Old Water Tower), and Bissell Street Water Tower. It was not, however, until 1904 that the city, under pressure from the organizers of the Louisiana Purchase Exposition who wanted clear water for planned fountains, the Grand Basin and lagoons, introduced the use of calcium carbonate to remove impurities that had made St. Louis water brown during the nineteenth century.

The city continued to expand to the west after the war. The elite of the city abandoned downtown and moved to several exclusive neighborhoods to the west.

Henry Shaw, a successful businessman, created one of the lasting St. Louis institutions, the Missouri Botanical Garden, or Shaw's Garden. After he made his fortune selling hardware and investing in real estate, Shaw retired at the ripe old age of thirty-nine. His travels abroad inspired him to create a public garden for St. Louis.

Citizens worried that much of St. Louis' history was being forgotten or destroyed joined together to create the Missouri Historical Society, still a vibrant institution today.

Compton Heights

Bounded by Grand, Russell, Geyer, Nebraska, Hawthorne and Longfellow Streets

At the turn of the twentieth century, a new planned residential development opened southwest of downtown and eventually attracted the movers and shakers of St. Louis society and business at the time. Compton Heights was a part of the land known as St. Louis Commons during colonial days. In 1888, thirty-three St. Louis businessmen formed the Compton Hill Improvement Company (CHIC), investing $400,000 at $100 per share, divided it into lots and proceeded to develop the properties with some unique twists.

Two of the investors had a huge influence on the community's development, Henry C. Haarstick and Julius Pitzman. Haarstick was the main developer, eventually holding a majority of the shares in the CHIC. He arrived in St. Louis from Germany at the age of thirteen in 1849, one of the worst years in the city's history, due to the fire that destroyed most of downtown and a cholera epidemic that took 10 percent of the city's population. Still, he made his first fortune by the age of thirty-one by investing in, then selling, a distillery. He used that money to buy the city's only barge line, St. Louis and Mississippi Valley Transportation, and turned it into the largest barge line in the United States. At the time, he controlled all trade coming from the west on the Mississippi River and extended his reach internationally. Haarstick also invested in chemicals and banking, further increasing his fortune.

Julius Pitzman may be the most famous surveyor in St. Louis history, and he had a visible influence on the development of Compton Heights. After the Civil War, he set out to survey the entirety of St. Louis County and by 1878 had published *Pitzman's New Atlas of the City and County of St. Louis, Missouri*. Even today, it's looked at as one of the most detailed and accurate surveys of the time. His first project was Benton Place in Lafayette Square, believed to be the first private street in the nation. Vandeventer Place followed, replicating the grand tree-lined boulevards with spacious lots for St. Louisans who could afford them. His vision changed when it came time to lay out Compton Heights.

Compton Heights was distinct from prior developments in two ways. First, Pitzman designed curved streets to take advantage of the natural layout of the landscape—in his words, to "view nature as a neighbor not as an enemy." Second, Compton Heights was the first development in Missouri to attach deed restrictions to the lots the company sold. These restrictions still apply to any lot originally sold by Compton Hill Improvement Company. They state that each lot can have only one building and it must be a private residence and had to cost between $3,000 and $8,000, depending on the lot. Setback requirements, measured from the street, required that no part of the building be closer than ten feet to the side of the lot. The restrictions continue to apply to subsequent buyers. Though these rules are restrictive, the neighborhood believes they saved Compton Heights when the surrounding area turned large houses into multifamily dwellings.

The development did not take off immediately, and remaining lots were ultimately sold at auction. Still, wealthy community leaders bought lots and built homes in the area. Many were German immigrants, and their influence can be seen in the details of the homes, such as arches and castle-like turrets. Once the lots were sold, CHIC dissolved, so no organization was left to enforce the regulations. However, residents took it upon themselves to do so, and there is still an active neighborhood association, Compton Heights Neighborhood Betterment Association.

The Magic Chef Mansion is an excellent example of the architecture and story of Compton Heights. This magnificent home was built in 1908 for Charles Stockstrom. The house was designed by Ernst Janssen, who designed more than twelve of the homes in the neighborhood as well as the entrance pillars on Grand Boulevard. Janssen designed mansions for so many beer barons that his eclectic style is sometimes referred to as "Beer Baronial." The Stockstroms lived in the mansion until his death in 1935, when it passed to his daughter Adda Ohlmeyer who died in 1990. At that time, the furniture and fixtures were sold at public auction and the house was sold to its current owner, who restored it.

Charles Stockstrom was born in Germany and immigrated to the United States about 1867. His brother-in-law invited him to join the Ringen Stove Company in 1881, where Stockstrom made his fortune. The company created the Quick Meal Stove, an ornate, enameled cooking stove. It was promoted with the slogan, "They drive drudgery from the kitchen and make happy homes. They are a boon to womankind. THAT'S WHAT THEY ARE." With the success of Ringen and Quick Meal, the companies joined with six other cookstove manufacturers and distributors to form the American Stove Company. That company patented the Lorain valve, the first stove device to allow the cook to set

The Compton Hill Water Tower is one of only three that still stand in St. Louis. The tower has been refurbished and is open for visitors on limited dates. *St. Louis Landmarks.*

an accurate temperature on a gas range. This valve revolutionized cook stoves and made the American Stove Company and Magic Chef a leading stove manufacturer in the world. Its plant employed as many as two thousand people in St. Louis.

The twelve-thousand-square-foot home features a stained-glass window in the main hall depicting the Stockstrom family coat of arms. In the library an elk mounted by Schwartz Taxidermy in 1923 was restored by the same company in 1991. The oval dining room has a restored hand-printed frieze and stencils. A cypress bench in the conservatory had been relegated to the basement in pieces but was reassembled by the current owner. One of the interesting features is the bowling alley in the basement. Pins must be hand-set, and the alley has a rare aboveground ball return. The mansion is open limited days for tours.

One of the key landmarks of Compton Heights is the water tower in Compton Heights Reservoir Park. The tower, located at Grand and Russell, was a popular tourist attraction during the 1904 World's Fair and continues to attract visitors today. It was designed by Harvey Ellis in 1894 and is 179 feet tall with 198 steps, offering a lovely view of the city. Constructed of limestone, buff brick and terra-cotta, it cost $48,000. This tower is open limited days and times to the public. It is one of seven surviving water towers out of more than five hundred in the United States and one of three in St. Louis. The water towers delivered water to St. Louis residents in the late nineteenth and early twentieth centuries. Steam-driven pumps delivered the water from plants to homes and businesses. The purpose of the standpipe was to absorb surges from water pumps to keep water pressure steady—in other words, to keep pipes from exploding. The towers were beautiful, but they also offered protection to the inner workings. The water delivery system was a factor in the city's expansion as well as a source of pride. Residents no longer had to rely on cisterns or wells for their water.

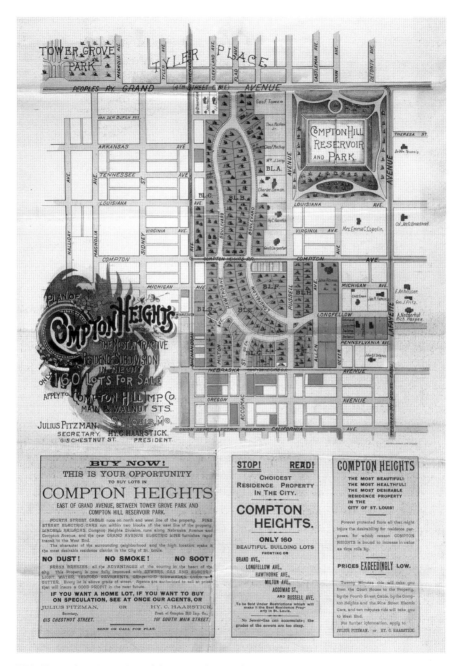

This illustration shows the original plan for the Compton Heights subdivision. *Missouri Historical Society.*

Another of the three towers is located at North Grand Boulevard and Twenty-Second Street. It was designed by George I. Barnett, who also designed the Old Courthouse, Henry Shaw's Tower Grove House and the Missouri Governor's Mansion. The tower is also known as Water Tower #1, the White Tower and the Old Water Tower. It is 154 feet tall, the pipe is 5 feet in diameter and it cost $35,530.39 to build. It is the oldest of the towers, built in 1871. After it was replaced by a pump system, the tower was used as an aviation beacon. It is the tallest freestanding Corinthian column in the world.

The Bissell Street Water Tower is located at Bissell and Blair Streets. It was designed by William S. Eames. Built in 1885–86, it cost $79,798. The brick, stone and terra-cotta tower was taken out of service in 1912. It is 194 feet, 8 inches tall with a 6-foot diameter. It is the tallest of the three towers and was restored in the 1970s. It is sometimes referred to as the New Red Tower.

Due to technological advances, the tower was taken out of use in 1929. In 1995, there were plans to demolish the structure, but residents banded together to save it, restoring it in 1999. Today, it is maintained by the Water Tower and Park Preservation Society.

Forest Park

Between Lindell and Oakland Avenues
St. Louis, MO 63112

Forest Park, created in 1874 by the Missouri legislature and opened on June 24, 1876, is one of the biggest urban parks in the nation. It encompasses 1,300 acres, making it larger even than Central Park in New York City. Today, the park welcomes over twelve million visitors a year. There is much to see, including monuments, historic buildings, wildlife, waterways, landscapes and attractions like the St. Louis Zoo, the St. Louis Art Museum, Missouri History Museum, the Science Center, the Muny Opera, the Boathouse, Steinberg Skating Rink, Dwight Davis Tennis Center and Probstein and Highlands Golf Courses. The park also hosts activities such as baseball, cycling, fishing, soccer, rugby, running, walking and simply enjoying the sights.

Today, the park is owned and operated by the City of St. Louis. When opened, the location was in St. Louis County (the city was part of the county at that time), two miles from the city limits and a forty-minute carriage ride from downtown. It was farmland on the Missouri Pacific Railroad line and was reached by traveling on dirt roads. The name derived from the virgin forest that composed a part of the lands selected for the park.

In the beginning, Forest Park was a response to the effects of the bad air created by the Industrial Revolution and offered a respite from the city with plenty of fresh country air. The park was accessible by carriage and public transportation and featured nineteen miles of gravel roads.

Soon after the park's opening in 1876, St. Louis City split from St. Louis County, leading to budget restraints. The park resided in the city limits. However, in the decade between 1880 and 1890, the park developed its own nursery for plants and landscaping as well as a fishery that provided fish to bodies of water across the state. The Forest Park Hatchery today has five of the original nine ponds. The Missouri Department of Conservation uses the hatchery for educational programming.

In 1894, the *St. Louis Post-Dispatch* raised $19,000 in donations to build and expand the lake now known as Post-Dispatch Lake. Employment had taken a blow because of an economic crash, so the creation also offered much-needed jobs. Soon after, in 1896, an amusement park, Forest Park Highlands, was built south of the park. Besides the regular amusement park offerings, the Highlands featured a theater and a swimming pool. It was destroyed by fire in 1963. Around the same time, people began building homes on private streets nearby and in the Central West End, with homes and shops developed at the north and east ends of the park.

By 1894, seven streetcar lines provided transportation to the park for its 2.5 million annual visitors. There were two pavilions near the stops, one on Lindell and one at Laclede. The Lindell pavilion burned in 1924 but was rebuilt and now houses the education center. The Laclede pavilion was demolished in 1938. Today's Dennis and Judith Jones Visitor and Education Center houses offices and one of five Explore St. Louis Visitor Centers located throughout the city.

Of course, one of the high points for both Forest Park and St. Louis was the 1904 Louisiana Purchase Exposition, also known as the St. Louis World's Fair or the 1904 World's Fair. Twenty million people visited the fairgrounds, a wonderland of buildings and exhibits. After all the celebrating, it took seven years to rebuild the park. The only buildings remaining from the fair are the St. Louis Art Museum and the 1904 Flight Cage. The World's Fair Pavilion, often believed to be a remnant from 1904, was built as a monument to the event. The Turtle Monument nearby is in memory of Myron Glassberg, a patron of St. Louis parks who funded the renovation of the pavilion. A tradition started on January 8, 1905, that exists to the present day. On that day, after a snowstorm, workers at the park rode folding chairs down Art Hill, the incline that connects the St. Louis Art Museum to the Grand Basin. Today, the hill is still the site of excellent sledding for St. Louisans.

The Grand Basin was the center of the St. Louis World's Fair and lined with temporary buildings. Today, it is called Emerson Grand Basin and creates a vista perfect for photographs.

Dwight F. Davis was named park commissioner in 1911. He was a proponent of recreation and athletics, leading to a new era concentrating on activities available in the park. As commissioner, he built the first official public golf course in St. Louis, in 1912. Originally nine holes, the course was expanded to eighteen, then nine more holes were added. He also had thirty-two public tennis courts created, not surprising, as Davis played tennis in the 1904 Olympics and founded an international tennis competition whose award, the Davis Cup, is named after him.

After three years of arguing over a location, Mayor Henry Kiel signed legislation authorizing a zoo on seventy acres in Forest Park. The zoo has been a major attraction in the park since then, known internationally not only for its exhibits but for also its research and sustenance of wild species.

In 1917, a fundraising effort for an outdoor theater in the park was initiated. It was a response to a successful outdoor performance of Shakespeare's *As You Like It* in 1916. Funds from the Pageant and Masque of St. Louis celebrating the city's sesquicentennial financed that performance. The Municipal Opera's first performance was on June 16, 1919, making St. Louis the first major city with an outdoor theater. The concept has been duplicated many times over since that night in other cities. During the 1919 season, Muny officials offered free seats on the grass, still a Muny tradition, although actual seats are now offered.

For less than a year, a portion of the park was turned into a landing field for airmail service in 1918. After that, the airfield served private planes and exhibition flights. The hangar for the field is now the headquarters for the St. Louis Mounted Police. The field itself has been converted to baseball and softball diamonds.

St. Louis welcomed Charles Lindbergh back to the city following his transatlantic flight in the *Spirit of St. Louis* on June 19, 1927. Over one hundred thousand people turned out for another major event that took place in Forest Park.

The Jewel Box, an indoor botanical exhibit housed in glass, opened on November 14, 1936, partly financed by WPA funds. It is a popular spot for weddings. A statue of St. Francis of Assisi, the patron saint of animals, stands near the Jewel Box in a butterfly garden. The statue was erected in memory of Harry Turner by his wife, Alice, and promotes Turner's belief that St. Louis would be a better place if it reflected the teachings of St. Francis, who gave up a life of wealth to live in poverty and peace.

During World War II, the park was a recreational camp for white soldiers on leave. As a result of segregation, after the war, Forest Park worked to desegregate. The idea received support from a large donation by Etta E. Steinberg to build the Mark C. Steinberg Memorial Skating Rink in 1955. The donor attached a condition to this, the single largest donation to Forest Park up to that time, that the rink be opened to all, making it one of the only integrated venues in the city at the time. The rink opened in 1957. It is the Midwest's largest outdoor ice rink and only uses real ice. This means the rink is open only in winter. Etta Steinberg also donated a statue called *Joie de Vivre* by Jacques Lipchitz to the park, and it makes its home at the rink.

In the 1980s, Forest Park began to show signs of its age. In 1986, Forest Park Forever, a private, nonprofit organization, was created to work with the city to improve the park. Park attractions are also part of the Metropolitan Zoological Park and Museum District, via a property tax originally supporting the St. Louis Zoo, Art Museum and Science Center. It expanded to include the Missouri History Museum and the Missouri Botanical Garden as well.

Besides the museums and the zoo, Forest Park has other sights of historical interest. Take note of the bronze plates set in the sidewalks throughout the park. They offer factoids about the history.

The statue of Edward Bates is the first statue erected in the park. Bates was a lawyer in St. Louis and also served in state government and as a member of the U.S. House of Representatives. He was a member of Missouri's state constitutional convention and served as a member of the Missouri House of Representatives and Missouri Senate. Bates served as U.S. attorney general under Abraham Lincoln during the Civil War.

The Musicians Memorial, a bronze relief of the Greek god Pan, was erected in 1930. The fountain in front of it was restored in honor of KMOX personality Jack Carney.

Flegel Falls, across from the Probstein Golf Course, mimics the St. Louis World's Fair Cascades. The falls were built by the WPA in the 1930s and are the origin of the park's river system.

The Boathouse dates to 1894. It is a restaurant as well as a site to rent paddleboats, paddleboards, canoes and kayaks. Paddle out to Wildlife Island, the home to many species of native Missouri wildlife and plants.

The Friedrich Jahn Memorial honors the German gymnastics instructor and founder of the Turnverein, a gymnastics and social society of the same name. The forty-one-foot-long statue dates to 1913 and was funded by the North American Turn Bund, a German cultural society.

A Spanish cannon named the Examinador, or Inspector, makes its home along Lindell Boulevard. The cannon saw action during the Spanish-American War and came to St. Louis in early 1900. Because there was no money to

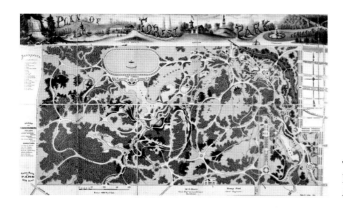

The original plan for Forest Park. *Missouri Historical Society.*

display the cannon, it was housed in the mounted police headquarters. Following a *St. Louis Post-Dispatch* article written as an interview with the cannon and bemoaning its residence with the horses, the cannon was moved to its present location. In 2010, when a Forest Park volunteer solved the mystery of its beginnings, a sign was erected explaining the cannon's significance.

The Cabanne House, formerly a home to park superintendents and commissioners, was the first brick farmhouse west of the Mississippi River. Restored in 2006, it is available for event rentals.

The original Korean War Memorial, dating to 1951, was a floral clock. It deteriorated over time. The present memorial, a sundial, replaced it in 1989. Two granite tablets memorialize the names of the 258 men and women from St. Louis who died in the war.

Franz Sigel was a German American leader of pro-Union forces in the St. Louis immigrant community. He served as a military commander during the Civil War. His statue is the first equestrian statue erected in St. Louis. The statue is a reminder of the heroism and patriotism of German Americans during that war.

Below the World's Fair Pavilion at the bottom of the hill in a grove of pine trees sits *PINE*, a sculpture honoring the recipients of the St. Louis Award. The award goes to a "resident of metropolitan St. Louis who, during the preceding year, has contributed the most outstanding service for its development."

Missouri History Museum

5700 Lindell Boulevard
St. Louis, MO 63112
After the Civil War, Elihu Shepard petitioned city leaders to join him in forming a historical society to save the early history of Missouri and St. Louis, but especially St. Louis. After 270 people signed, a group met at the Old

Courthouse to officially establish the Missouri Historical Society on August 11, 1866. For twenty years, the society met at members' homes and other locations to hear lectures. In the 1880s, the organization set out to collect artifacts as well. Their collection was so successful that it soon overwhelmed the storage space the society had available. The Thomas Larken mansion in downtown St. Louis became available in 1886, and it became the headquarters of the historical society. It wasn't until 1892, when membership decreased and finances became an issue, that the exhibits opened to public viewing.

Many of the people active in the Missouri Historical Society (MHS) were also active in organizing the St. Louis World's Fair. This interest in collecting and preserving history led to a push for using a portion of the fair's profits to build the Jefferson Memorial Building, a permanent home for the Missouri History Museum and a monument to Thomas Jefferson. The Jefferson Memorial opened on April 30, 1913, with over 230,000 people in attendance.

With Lettie Beauregard as curator and Stella Drumm as librarian, the museum acquired significant additions to its collection, including artifacts from the Lewis and Clark expedition and memorabilia from Charles Lindbergh. Exhibits of the Lindbergh memorabilia led to a surge in visitors to the museum. Miss Lettie, as she was known, was a force in collecting, archiving, installing exhibits, greeting guests and, with Stella Drumm's help, doing the work of what it takes many more employees to do today.

The south entrance to the Missouri History Museum opens to a recent expansion that doubled the space available. *Author photo.*

The north entrance facing Lindell Boulevard is the original facade of the Missouri History Museum. *St. Louis Landmarks.*

William Clark's descendant Julia Clark Voorhis was hounded by many museums that desired to possess Clark's artifacts from his journey. Miss Lettie used her social connections to schedule tea with Julia, and that led to a donation of the William Clark Collection to the society.

Lettie Beauregard also made a personal connection with Charles Lindbergh, whose transatlantic flight was financed by St. Louis businessmen, some of whom were members of the MHS Board. She had a promise from him, before the attempt, that if it was successful, he would donate the trophies and awards given to him after the flight to the museum. She spent much of her time working with the Lindbergh collection, which expanded to include other memorabilia. Lindbergh even took Miss Lettie on a plane ride over St. Louis.

Of course, subsequent curators were equally successful in acquiring donations, but Miss Lettie was the first. She created a strong foundation for those who followed to build upon.

In 1925, the Missouri Historical Society merged with the Louisiana Purchase Historical Association, and the mission broadened to include materials about the Louisiana Purchase and westward expansion.

In 1987, facing, as all museums do, financial woes, MHS joined the Metropolitan Zoological Park and Museum District, meaning it received of a portion of taxes collected on behalf of the district.

After an expansion in 2000, the society decided to focus on local history, leading to some of its most popular exhibits.

Today, the Missouri Historical Society includes three locations: the original Missouri History Museum, the Library and Research Center (1991) and Soldiers Memorial (2015). In addition to exhibits showcasing the history of St. Louis, they offer educational programs, research opportunities and special events.

Missouri Historical Society Library and Research Center

225 South Skinker Boulevard
St. Louis, MO 63105

The former home of the United Hebrew Congregation (UHC) was dedicated as the Missouri Historical Society Library and Research Center in 1991. The facility's fifty-four-thousand square feet houses, preserves and protects the society's collections. It is also a functioning library available for research and as a genealogical resource.

In 1837, the United Hebrew Congregation became the first Jewish congregation in St. Louis, as well as the first west of the Mississippi River. It was the twentieth congregation in the United States. The congregation worshipped in a number of places until the building that now belongs to the MHS Library was designed and built as a Byzantine-style synagogue by Gabriel Ferrand of Maritz and Young. The facility opened in 1927 and remained the home of the congregation until 1989, when UHC moved to a new synagogue in Chesterfield.

After a renovation, the research library opened in 1991. There are four levels of storage, and the reading room is the former sanctuary. The same room was the site of a speech by Martin Luther King Jr. in 1960 on "The Future of Integration." The speech was part of the Liberal Forum series sponsored by the Jewish Community Center. Due to the response to the announcement of Dr. King's speech, organizers knew they needed a bigger space for attendees, and the event was moved to United Hebrew Congregation

By the numbers, the library contains more than 1,000,000 photos and prints, more than 175,000 artifacts, over 100,000 library volumes and 7,900 linear feet of documents. Some of these items are available for online viewing, and more are added all the time. Artifacts in the collection include the William Clark Collection, donations from Charles Lindbergh, 1904 World's Fair memorabilia and artifacts, textiles and Thomas Jefferson papers. The library is open to the public, although some research may require appointments.

Missouri Botanical Garden

4344 Shaw Boulevard

St. Louis, MO 63110

The Missouri Botanical Garden, the invention of Henry Shaw, is still referred to as Shaw's Garden by many St. Louisans, in honor of the founder. And it started out as Shaw's personal garden.

Henry Shaw arrived in St. Louis on May 4, 1819, traveling a rather roundabout route from England. He and his father first came to Canada. His father borrowed money to send a shipment of goods on consignment to New Orleans, where he had a partner who was supposed to sell them. The partner failed to take care of business, and Henry's father fled his creditors. Shaw made his way to New Orleans, found the merchandise and traveled upriver to St. Louis, arriving at the right moment. The tools in the shipment were exactly what was needed, and he created a successful hardware business selling to soldiers, farmers and westward-bound settlers as well as St. Louisans. He invested wisely, especially in real estate both in and outside the city, retiring at the ripe old age of thirty-nine. He built a country home he called Tower Grove House after the view visitors saw as they approached the property, the house's tower rising above a grove of trees.

While traveling abroad, Shaw became inspired by the gardens he viewed on grand estates in Europe and determined to create his own. After his final trip to England to visit the London World's Fair in 1851, Shaw returned to St. Louis to turn his idea into reality.

Shaw consulted some of the greatest botanical and naturalist minds in the world while planning his gardens. Writing first to Sir William Jackson Hooker, director of the Royal Botanic Gardens at Kew, he was referred to an amateur botanist in St. Louis, Dr. George Engelmann, who also was one of the founders of St. Louis Academy of Science. Asa Gray of Harvard University, the country's leading naturalist, also joined the team. The three experts convinced Shaw to create not simply a garden that served as a park but one that included a research element, like a zoo for plants. The garden expanded to include a library, a museum and sixty thousand species of plants from the collection of a German botanist. Today, the garden has over five million plant specimens and over 120,000 volumes in its library.

While Henry Shaw created his botanical garden, the still unmarried man met a woman, Effie Carstang, while strolling in the garden, and they became friends. Effie borrowed money from him several times and rented a piano from Shaw for $1 per month. When Shaw took the piano back, she claimed it had been a gift and that Shaw had promised to marry her. She was thirty years old;

Shaw was sixty. In November 1856, Effie sued Shaw for $100,000 for breach of promise. At the trial, Effie testified that Shaw had sent her gifts, including the piano, which he then took back, giving as an excuse that he needed it for a party at his home. He then stopped visiting her. She called on him, thinking he might be ill, and he made an indecent proposal. The court ruled in favor of Effie for the entire $100,000. Because of the size of the award, the case made national news. On appeal, Shaw's defense attacked Effie's character, claiming bad conduct on her part and that she had sued others for breach of promise. They also accused her of bad conduct in church (she smiled during the sermon) and that she made the acquaintance of Shaw only to entrap him. The verdict was overturned, fortunately for the garden. The sum of money awarded (then taken away) would have impacted the development of the project. Henry Shaw never married and considered the garden his love.

The garden opened on June 15, 1859, along with the Museum Building, housing the library and the herbarium with its collection of plant specimens. Henry Shaw oversaw the garden until his death thirty years later.

In 1885, he founded the Henry Shaw School of Botany at Washington University in lieu of agreeing to turn over the garden to the university at his death. Under the agreement, the school had access to the research facilities at the garden and the head of the school would also be an employee of the garden. The first professor was William Trelease, who became director of the botanical garden after Shaw's death. He and his family moved into Shaw's home and expanded it to make it more comfortable for a family. The house is open, with some original furnishings, on limited days and hours.

In Shaw's time, the garden had a farm, a formal European-style garden (known as a parterre), an arboretum, an observation tower, a conservatory and the Linnean House. Many of these gardens and structures no longer exist, but the Linnean House is still there. It is the oldest continuously operating greenhouse west of the Mississippi River. Today, it houses the botanical garden's collection of camellias.

Henry Shaw's health began to decline in the late 1880s, and he died on August 25, 1889. Shaw lay in state at the Museum Building, where many St. Louisans paid their respects. In addition to the garden, Shaw also gave the city Tower Grove Park and was a supporter of the Missouri Historical Society and the St. Louis Mercantile Library. He is buried on the garden grounds in a mausoleum he designed that features a statue he posed for himself, reclining.

At his death, the Missouri Botanical Garden became a charitable trust governed by a board of trustees. He wanted his garden to exist for research and the public's enjoyment for all time.

Above: The geodesic dome design of the Climatron was an innovation at the time it was built. The pond in front of the building shows some of the lilies that the Missouri Botanical Garden has developed, as well as sculptures from an exhibit by Dale Chihuly. *Author photo*.

Left: After Henry Shaw died, William Trelease, who took over as director of the Missouri Botanical Garden, expanded the home to make room for his family. The house is open to the public on limited days and hours. *Author photo*.

The Missouri Botanical Garden changes and grows with the times. It has had ups and downs with financial problems, natural disasters (in 1946, a tornado destroyed much of the outside of the garden), wars (part of the garden was turned into a Victory garden), the Depression and varied attendance.

Some of the highlights include the opening of the Climatron in 1960, a geodesic dome greenhouse. It was the first new project in fifty years at the garden and increased attendance. The Japanese Garden, a visitor favorite, opened in 1977. The scented garden for the visually impaired opened in 1983. A Chinese garden, a German garden, a rose garden, Piper Observatory (based on the observatory present in Shaw's time) and a Victorian garden have also been added, as well as services and programs.

St. Louis Public Library

1301 Olive Street
St. Louis, MO 63103

In 1865, Ira Divall, superintendent of the St. Louis Public Schools, established a subscription (fee-based) library called the Public School Library and Lyceum at Fifth and Olive. The library was developed as a supplement to the public school system and contained 1,500 volumes. A short time later, in 1869, the St. Louis School Board took control of the library and moved it to Seventh and Chestnut. In 1874, the library opened to the public for on-site use. There were no age restrictions, unusual for libraries at the time, and it was open twelve hours a day. The library had increased its holdings to 90,000 volumes by 1893, and it moved to the St. Louis Board of Education building at Ninth and Locust. That year, voters also moved the governance of the library to an independent board and approved a property tax, making it the library it is today: free and open to all St. Louis residents. The building was home to the library until 1909. It still stands and the top two floors of former "library" space are now loft apartments.

The library quickly outgrew the board of education building. Fortunately, an industrialist and library philanthropist was waiting in the wings to help. Andrew Carnegie attributed his success to having access to a private library during his youth. He wanted others to have the same opportunity. He put his money to work, funding over 1,600 public libraries in the United States, one of the largest philanthropic endeavors in history. To receive funding, an organization only had to provide land to build on and support for the library through taxes. In 1901, Carnegie made one of his largest donations: $1 million to the St. Louis Public Library—$500,000 to build a Central Library and $500,000 to build branches. The Central Library alone cost $1.5 million, made possible by supplemental local money.

Cass Gilbert (who also designed the building that would one day house the St. Louis Art Museum), one of the country's most famous architects, designed the library. Gilbert considered the Central Library to be one of his most important works.

Interestingly, the site for the new library was already occupied by a building that was just twenty years old: the St. Louis Exposition and Music Hall. The hall was the site of historic events itself, such as the nomination of President Grover Cleveland. It was torn down to make room for the library.

The original blueprints are available for visitors to view at Central Library, as are many photos of the construction, which took place from 1907 to 1909. Mattie Hewitt, who moved to New York soon after the library was complete, was one of the photographers. She went on to have a career in architectural photography in the East.

By the end of the twentieth century, the library was showing wear. A $70 million renovation began in 2010 and culminated in "historic spaces combined with...new construction within the existing historic shell" (AIA/ALA Library Building Awards Jury). Others called it a "work of art." Ron Charles, in an article in the *Washington Post*, said: "The results...are now open to the public and the 190,000 square foot building is the most gorgeous—and usable—library I have ever seen." It is a beautiful building with delightful artistic and architectural details, such as stained-glass and stenciled ceilings.

The St. Louis Public Library is one of the many public libraries funded by Andrew Carnegie. *Author photo.*

The exterior walls are granite from a quarry in Mount Waldo, Maine, and the renovation used granite from the same quarry in 2011. A massive stone staircase leads from Olive Street to the main entrance. The staircase is supported by Pittsburgh steel and features storage underneath. Because of the salt used to clear the stairs of ice and snow, the steel deteriorated to the point that the staircase became unsafe. During the restoration, the stone was removed and numbered. When new supports were in place, the stones were returned to their original locations. The building was improved and updated to better serve the almost three million annual visitors.

The St. Louis Public Library system has seventeen branches and 4.6 million items in the system.

Tower Grove Park

4256 Magnolia Avenue

St. Louis, MO 63110

Henry Shaw's second gift to the city of St. Louis was the land for Tower Grove Park. In 1868, he donated the land for the park to the city, but not without conditions. The land was to remain a park forever, and the city was to make an appropriation every year for maintenance and upkeep. Shaw had definite opinions about parks, believing they should serve "not only as ornaments to a great city, but as conducive to the health and happiness of its inhabitants and to the advancement of refinement and culture." Tower Grove Park is the only park in the city managed by an independent board of commissioners and staff. As a result, the park is a center for culture, education, athletics, play and nature.

Another of Shaw's beliefs was that sculpture was important in parks. Four full-size statues graced Tower Grove at one time. Baron Friedrich Wilhelm von Steuben was a Prussian military officer who turned the Continental Army into a fighting force during the Revolutionary War. His statue was originally cast for the 1904 World's Fair and moved to the park in 1968. A statue of Alexander von Humboldt, a German explorer, naturalist and geographer who traveled the Americas in the early nineteenth century and wrote extensively about them from what was then a modern scientific view, was erected in 1878. Shakespeare took up residence in 1878, and Columbus was installed in 1886. The statue of Columbus was removed in 2020.

Busts of famous composers surround the music pavilion: Wagner, Beethoven, Gounod, Mozart, Verdi and Rossini. All of the statuary, as well as the architecture, reflects Shaw's interest in the classics and European design.

Tower Grove Park was donated to the people of St. Louis by Henry Shaw. The carved busts surrounding the bandstand in the park were of Shaw's favorite composers. Regular band concerts are still held at the park. *Author photo.*

The Piper Palm House started life as a greenhouse and is currently an event venue, popular for weddings. The nearly identical Piper Plant House dates from 1885 and has been a greenhouse and a maintenance facility and now serves as the park office.

Of the three comfort stations in Tower Grove Park, what is known as the Old Comfort Station is the most historically significant. It was built in 1913 of materials from the East Gate Lodge.

The tennis center, built in 1931 and renovated in 1966, features nine hard surface courts, eight pickleball courts and three refurbished grass courts. The grass courts are the only public grass courts in the country.

The four entrances or "Gates" to the park are also excellent examples of the European influences favored by Shaw. The East Gate on Grand Boulevard was built in 1870–72. It was designed to be the entrance for vehicles. The two lions and two griffins were brought from Berlin, Germany, by Henry Shaw. This gate is the most elaborate. The West Gate (also built in 1870–72) on Kingshighway Boulevard is the only example of Gothic Revival architecture in Tower Grove Park. Featuring four towers, the larger are thirty-eight feet tall and the smaller fifteen feet. The North Gate opens off Magnolia Avenue and was built between 1870 and 1892 using materials from the lower floor of the

St. Louis Courthouse when it was renovated in 1870. The South Gate was originally designed as an entrance for pedestrian traffic coming from Arsenal Street. The gate is most similar to the Magnolia Avenue gate, using the same limestone and wrought-iron materials.

Tower Grove Park is meant to be an urban green space and features seven thousand trees with over 325 species, making it more diverse than any park in the United States. There are fifty-six display flower beds and twenty urns featuring twenty thousand plants every year. The water lily ponds show off a number of species, including the giant type, big enough for people to stand on. The Fountain Pond and Ruins is a favorite spot for wedding photos. The ruins along the pond are cut stone dating to 1873 from the Old Lindell House. The site is a favorite spot to visit.

You may attend concerts, lectures, a farmers market and art shows in Tower Grove Park. The Compton Heights Concert Band performs ten concerts at the Music Stand each year. The Music Stand dates from 1872 and was Henry Shaw's favorite place in the park. The busts surrounding it are of his favorite composers.

Hawken House

1155 South Rock Hill Road
Webster Groves, MO 63119

The Hawken House was built by Christopher Hawken in 1867. Hawken was the son of Jacob Hawken and nephew of Samuel Hawken. Jacob and Samuel made and sold muzzle-loading rifles beginning in 1815 from their shop on the St. Louis riverfront. The weapons were hand-made for such well-known frontiersmen as Jim Bridger and Kit Carson. The Hawken rifle was popular with mountain men and fur traders and became known as the Rocky Mountain Rifle or the Plains Rifle.

The Hawken House Museum houses many artifacts from the post–Civil War era. This beautiful Greek Revival home is operated by the Webster Groves Historical Society. Tours are available.

Samuel Cupples House

3673 West Pine Mall
St. Louis, MO 63106

The Samuel Cupples House, completed in 1890, stands on the campus of St. Louis University. It houses a museum and a gallery of fine and decorative

Samuel Cupples built this home in 1890 after making a fortune in real estate. The house is now an art museum located on the campus of St. Louis University. *St. Louis Landmarks*.

art, both open to the public. It was placed in the National Register of Historic Places in 1976. It has forty-two rooms and twenty-two fireplaces. The first floor was devoted to entertainment spaces; the family lived on the second and third floors.

Cupples was a St. Louis businessman who came to the city at the age of fifteen. He distributed and manufactured wooden utensils and became a millionaire by the age of thirty through his dealings in real estate. From 1894 to 1917, he built a series of eighteen warehouses, known as the Cupples Station Complex, between Seventh and Eleventh Streets, next to the city's many railroad lines and had spurs built into the structures. This increased the efficiency for shippers by eliminating the need to transport goods from their warehouses to the railroad. It was a revolutionary idea that was eventually copied in New York, Chicago and Pittsburgh. Ten of the eighteen warehouses still stand. Several have been repurposed as a hotel, lofts and apartments. Cupples Station is also in the National Register of Historic Places.

St. Louis Union Station

1820 Market Street

St. Louis, MO 63103

The first train arrived at St. Louis Union Station on September 1, 1894, at 1:45 p.m. At that time, the station was the largest in the world with train tracks and passenger service on one level. The station was divided into three areas: the Headhouse, the Midway and the Train Shed. The Headhouse featured the hotel, a restaurant, waiting rooms for passengers and railroad ticket offices. The hotel was modest, with seventy-five rooms catering mostly to railroad employees, businessmen and some travelers. The rooms were small, sparsely furnished and shared a communal bathroom. The Grand Hall was the primary waiting room. Its features included gold leaf trim, Romanesque arches, a vaulted ceiling, stained-glass windows, two tons of wrought iron and a chandelier with 350 lights. One of the most well-known windows is the Allegorical Window. Three women are depicted in three windows, representing the expanse of 1890s travel, New York to St. Louis to San Francisco. The clock tower looming over the station is 230 feet tall. The Midway platform had wrought-iron gates, giving a view of the trains. The Train Shed covered 11.5 acres of ground and was the largest single-span train shed ever constructed. Its thirty-two tracks were more than any other U.S. station. The station was designed by St. Louis architect Theodore Link and cost $6.5 million.

Traffic during the 1904 World's Fair was surpassed only by military men and women and travelers during World War II, which reached a peak of over 100,000 passengers a day. The two tons of wrought iron in the station disappeared at this time, donated to the war effort.

As trains were replaced by cars and airplanes, there was no longer a need for a grand train station. The last train came to Union Station on October 31, 1978, at 11:38 p.m.

Many famous persons traveled in and out of Union Station, including Joe DiMaggio, Joan Crawford and Harry Truman. The famous photo of Truman holding a copy of the *Chicago Tribune* misstating "Dewey Defeats Truman" was taken at Union Station as the president set off for Washington, D.C.

Fortunately, although there was no longer a need for a train station, the architectural and historical significance of Union Station led to a reincarnation of the site. It reopened in 1985 with shops, an event space, restaurants and a hotel with 539 rooms/suites and a railroad theme. The Grand Hall retained its original terrazzo floors, the green glazed terra-cotta bricks and the stained-glass windows.

Union Station is a St. Louis landmark. Once a train station, it is now a hotel, meeting venue and entertainment site. The clock tower at one time held over thirty thousand gallons of water for use in case of fire. *Creative Commons.*

But the focus and activities have changed. There is a light show set to music in the Grand Hall every evening at 5:00 p.m. There are also fire and light shows at the lake.

After a setback with the attempt at retail, Union Station has a new life. There is a two-hundred-foot Ferris wheel, the St. Louis Wheel, with forty-two enclosed gondolas, each with seating for eight, and one VIP gondola with leather seats, a stereo system and a glass floor. The wheel offers spectacular views of the city and surrounds. There is also a carousel, if one prefers to stay on the ground.

St. Louis Aquarium now fills what was once the 120,000-square-foot mall area. It offers thirteen thousand animals and 250,000 gallons of water. A 90,000-cubic-foot ropes and zip line course soars over three stories at Union Station.

Scott Joplin House State Historic Site

2658 Delmar Boulevard
St. Louis, MO 63103
The building located at 2658 Delmar Boulevard in St. Louis was the home of Scott Joplin, the "King of Ragtime," from 1901 to 1903. Joplin was born in

Texas in 1868 into a musical family. His mother and father played instruments, and he learned piano at the home of his mother's employer. He was also accomplished in playing cornet and violin and as a singer.

Joplin moved to Sedalia, Missouri, in 1894, after working at the 1893 Chicago World's Fair. While there, he worked as a piano teacher and as a traveling musician. He also attended George R. Smith College to study music and to learn to transcribe his compositions so other musicians could play his songs. In 1899, he achieved a measure of national fame after composing the "Maple Leaf Rag." (Ragtime is defined as having a ragged, offbeat time with African American roots.)

He moved to St. Louis in 1901, along with his wife and several of his musician friends. As a group, they made the city the center of ragtime. Joplin also taught music and produced more rags, as well as several more serious works of opera and a ballet. He received grand reviews and much praise for his work, but because of his race, he found it difficult to get backing for his serious compositions. During his St. Louis days, he composed the popular "The Entertainer" (featured in the movie *The Sting*) and "Cascades" for the 1904 World's Fair. Even though the fair was not welcoming to African Americans, Joplin entertained on the Pike, the fair's entertainment district.

While in St. Louis, Joplin's only child, a daughter, died. His marriage fell apart after that. He did marry again, but his second wife died after they'd been married only a short time. Scott Joplin left St. Louis for New York in 1907, hoping to find financial backing for his operas and serious compositions. He died in a mental institution in 1917, probably suffering from the effects of tertiary syphilis.

Ragtime and Scott Joplin played an important role in the music world. Joplin and his development of ragtime laid the groundwork for another essentially American music form: jazz.

The Scott Joplin House gives a glimpse into his life. The second-floor flat is furnished as it would been at the time the Joplins lived there. The Rosebud, a bar and gaming club, operated by Joplin's friend Tom Turpin, has been replicated as well. One of the highlights of the museum is a player piano, from which guests may listen to some of Joplin's many compositions.

Chapter 7

WHEN THE WORLD CAME TO ST. LOUIS

1904 LOUISIANA PURCHASE EXPOSITION

I t's a locally accepted truth that the Louisiana Purchase Exposition, more commonly referred to in St. Louis as the 1904 or St. Louis World's Fair, was a high point for the city. It was a time when the world, 19.7 million paid visitors, came to the city.

The idea of a world's fair was initiated in London in 1851, leading to a proliferation of such events at the turn of the century. The first official World's Fair hosted in the United States was the Centennial Exposition in Philadelphia in 1876 to celebrate the one-hundredth anniversary of the signing of the Declaration of Independence. Although the fairs' purposes were nominally to promote peace and provide education, they also had a competitive edge: to promote trade and expand overseas empires. The fairs combined the ideas of a trade fair wrapped in a spectacle to provide entertainment. It was an opportunity for visitors to escape reality, see the wonders of the world and look to the future. The 1904 World's Fair was all that.

Led by David R. Francis, a former mayor of St. Louis and governor of Missouri, the Louisiana Purchase Exposition celebrated the centennial of the Louisiana Purchase. It was originally scheduled for 1903 but delayed a year due to construction difficulties.

Forest Park was selected as the ideal location for the fair. It had trees to provide shade and a backdrop for the planned buildings. It had water pressure and was surrounded by the best neighborhoods the city had to offer with impressive homes and open landscapes. However, the River Des Peres, which wandered through the location, was dirty and prone to flooding. After some wrangling with park officials, half of the park was leased to the exposition. Additional acreage was acquired surrounding the park. The River Des Peres was shortened, straightened and placed underground. What most fairgoers didn't know was that they were walking on water channeled underneath the paths. Ultimately, the fair cost $50 million to build.

The world fairs always had missions, both stated and unstated. The Louisiana Purchase Exposition was of course a way to celebrate expansionism. It also promoted the idea of St. Louis as the capital of the American West. Education was an important element in the planning and exhibits, as it was believed that education was the key to progress.

Expansionism, for example, was presented to visitors by exhibits in anthropology meant to illustrate theories of race that made it OK to expand the reach of a nation and take over those cultures. For example, a culture with no technological advances was viewed as inferior. Tribal peoples from around the world were exhibited to uphold this belief. A large display of peoples from the Philippines had the underlying principle of making a case for American presence in the islands as well as encouraging American investment in them.

The buildings, in the interest of time and money, were made of staff, a mixture of plaster of paris and hemp fibers placed on wood frames. The staff was molded, hoisted onto the frames and nailed into position. The staff could then be painted, although nearly all of the buildings at the fair were painted white.

Although some of the Palaces, as they were called, covered expanses equal to city blocks, they were demolished at fair's end. The only building that remained, the only one built to be a permanent addition to Forest Park, was what is now the St. Louis Art Museum. Countries and museums sending precious and valuable artwork to the 1904 World's Fair wanted it to be safe, especially from fire, the scourge of the times. By being constructed as a permanent structure, the Palace of Fine Arts assured donors their artwork would be protected.

There were twelve major Palaces covering 135 acres and costing $6,449,736 to erect. The Louisiana Purchase Exposition Company received a commission on everything sold at the fair, resulting in a profit of approximately $850,000. It was the only World's Fair to make money. What were some of these Palaces, and what treasures did they hold?

One of the most photographed structures was the Festival Hall. This was a place to hear great music and to view the world's largest pipe organ (one of

One of the most beautiful buildings at the 1904 World's Fair was Festival Hall. *Missouri Historical Society.*

three organs in the hall). It sat atop a hill with water flanking it, known as the Cascades. The waterfalls represented the Atlantic and Pacific Oceans. The water flowed into the Grand Basin. The Colonnade of States, representing the thirteen states and Indian Territory (later Oklahoma) that were carved from the Louisiana Purchase, lined the Grand Basin.

First to be completed was the Palace of Varied Industries, presenting displays of industrial arts and covering fourteen acres. Products displayed included Persian rugs, jewelry, Japanese porcelain, pottery, cloisonne and ivory. Kimonos proved to be a popular purchase, selling out in two weeks. Larger items were held for delivery after the fair. Tinted lenses, a precursor to sunglasses, offered a way to see the world in a different color. Ingersoll Watch Company was the official timekeeper for the 1904 World's Fair and had booths not only in Varied Industries but also all over the grounds, offering watches at a variety of prices. There was a broom factory. One of the elements promoted by the fair was the illustration of the manufacturing process as well as the product, and exhibitors took it to heart. The Palace of Varied Industries also featured the world's largest barber chair.

The Palace of Manufacturers was known as the shopping center of the fair. Personal items such as clothes, household wares and jewelry could be easily purchased. It also featured demonstrations and displays in a flurry of life and motion. Hardware and textiles, cutlery, stoves, furnaces, sewing machines and clothing on live models were exhibited. Visitors could also view how shoes were made. Vacuum cleaners and washing machines were some of the more modern innovations introduced. One display made cardboard boxes on-site. These were then sold to retailers to use for purchases. At the end of the fair, the Palace of Manufacturers' exhibitors put many items on sale, pleasing fairgoers.

Theodore Roosevelt dedicated the Louisiana Purchase Exposition on April 30, 1903 (yes, the date is correct), from the Palace of Liberal Arts. It covered nine acres and displayed a printing press, demonstrated how perfume was made from flowers, photography, typewriters, even a lighthouse. This was the only Palace that had color on the exterior. Sweden's exhibit had a machine producing sulphur-headed matchsticks, filling a case with 135,000 matches every fifteen seconds. They were given out as souvenirs to visitors. France displayed Mucha Art Nouveau posters, still popular today. The N.K. Fairbanks Company (a soap manufacturer) built a twenty-two-foot-tall fountain with a statue of a fairy standing on soap bubbles. Bubbles cascaded down on visitors. In addition to the photography exhibits in the Palace of Liberal Arts, there were two hundred photo booths across the fairgrounds. The booths had no operators; subjects tripped the camera with a handheld device and received six miniature photos for twenty-five cents.

The Palace of Mines and Metallurgy displayed models of mines as well as products. Outside the building, cement mixing, brick making and coal mining were displayed. Rides took visitors through a working anthracite coal mine and a Crystal Cave that presented mineral wonders. Some of the displays, including these, throughout the fair charged an admission fee. Birmingham, Alabama, brought a fifty-six-foot tall, one-hundred-thousand-pound statue of Vulcan to the 1904 World's Fair. It is the world's largest iron statue and now resides in Birmingham as a major tourist attraction.

Education was a top priority at the Louisiana Purchase Exposition, and the Palace of Education and Social Economy was an important part of that mission. Each week, a classroom of students from St. Louis Public Schools would be on display, showing students at work. A Model Street showed an idealized view of the future with its Model City Hall and Hospital. Even the streets themselves showed various paving materials. Everything was an exhibit! One of the most interesting and well-attended displays in this Palace was that illustrating police methods. The French Bertillion system used physical measurements of body parts to predict criminal behaviors.

It was used to narrow down suspects in specific crimes. Visitors could have themselves measured for their criminal propensity. A three-room Rogue's Gallery showed a photo, description and history of every individual convicted of a crime in St. Louis since 1843. The more acceptable identification model of fingerprinting was also on display. Criminals apprehended on the fairgrounds were locked up in Model Jails and then tried in Model Courts.

The Palace of Electricity and Machinery was particularly important because electricity was a prime exhibit at the fair. Each evening the Palaces themselves would become "indescribably grand" when electricity illuminated them in all their glory. Thomas Edison was the chief consulting engineer for the fair and made several visits to check on his displays as well as the fair in general. The three-hundred-foot-tall DeForest Wireless Telegraph Tower sent stories to local St. Louis newspapers; another tower across the grounds sent them to Chicago. An elevator to the top of the tower gave visitors a chance to overlook not only the fairgrounds but also the city. Free telephones were placed throughout the building for fairgoers to call anywhere in the country. Obviously, the 1904 World's Fair was the best display of the use and possibilities of electricity.

The Palace of Machinery housed the fair's generator, which covered 180,000 feet, half the size of the building, and used five hundred tons of coal a day. The power required to run the 1904 World's Fair was two and a half times that used to light the streets of Chicago. Compared to actual horsepower, it would take fifty-four thousand horses stretched from St. Louis to Jefferson City (128 miles). The Cascade pumps drove 165 million gallons of water daily, 100 million gallons more than the City of St. Louis used during the same time.

The Palace of Transportation celebrated the one hundredth anniversary of the steam locomotive, and the hall was designed to look like a large train station. This was the first World's Fair to show off gasoline-powered automobiles, but with less focus than on trains. One of the most eye-catching displays was the two-hundred-thousand-pound *Spirit of the 20th Century* locomotive, which sat on a rotating platform. The fair also sponsored a contest with a $5,000 prize for anyone who could pilot a balloon airship from St. Louis to Washington, D.C. Of the two entries, one made it as far as St. Charles, Missouri, and the other flew two hundred miles into Illinois.

The Palace of Fine Arts was the only permanent Palace. St. Louis citizens wanted an art museum to raise the cultural status of the city, and exhibitors wanted a safe place for their artworks. The building design was simple to keep the cost within bounds. The building featured American artworks.

The Palace of Fine Arts was the only permanent building on the fairgrounds. This is a photo from the fair. *Missouri Historical Society.*

There were three additional buildings displaying art as well as sculpture. The exhibit showed off applied and decorative arts as well as fine art.

The Palace of Agriculture, the largest of the fair, consisted of three buildings: Horticulture, Forestry and Fish and Game. A floral clock stretched 1,600 feet in front of the Palace of Agriculture. These buildings showcased the importance of agriculture. There were products from fifteen countries and forty-two states, showing livestock, butter making, cheese making, pasteurization and more. A restaurant that used product from the working exhibits was available for mealtime. Whimsical and inventive displays included a Texas star woven in native grains and grasses and California's almond elephant. Missouri collaborated with other corn-producing states to build a 45-foot-tall corn palace. Pillsbury was among the private companies leasing space to showcase a product and gave out loaves of bread. Fish and Game provided a fully stocked lake where fairgoers could cast a line, as well as an aquarium.

One reason for the popularity of World's Fairs was because they gave people unable to afford to travel to foreign countries a chance to sample foreign cultures. The Palace of Nations was the home for twenty-one national pavilions, each having the opportunity to display historical national treasures for the world to admire. They sold products from their nations, and many had living quarters available for the leader of the nation if they visited the fair. The buildings were also a place to rest, especially for people from that nation. Some of the nations modeled their buildings on famous structures from their country: France's pavilion was a replica of the Grand Trianon at Versailles, England reproduced the Orangery in Kensington Garden,

Germany the Palace of Charlottenbury and Argentina the Pink Palace in Buenos Aires. Canada, at the time considered the last frontier in North America, offered free land to encourage immigration. Japan had multiple buildings and gardens that featured a look at traditional Japanese culture. Elsewhere, Japanese exhibits showed the country's modern achievements. Belgium had the largest foreign pavilion. Anheuser-Busch purchased it after the fair and used it as a glasswork building on its campus for a time.

The Plateau of States gathered the buildings sponsored from within the United States. The various state buildings also included living quarters for visiting governors and other officials. The Alaska Territory, Arizona Territory, New Mexico Territory and Indian Territory also had buildings. Again, some of the states duplicated historic buildings famous in their state and highlighted an event or person important to them. New Hampshire's building was based on Daniel Webster's birthplace. The New Jersey building was a reproduction of the Old Ford Tavern; the Texas building was in the shape of a five-pointed star. Virginia's contribution was Jefferson's Monticello reborn. After all, the fair was also a celebration of the man who instigated the Louisiana Purchase. Other buildings were given a second life after the fair. The Maine building was purchased by a group of hunters and moved to the Ozarks. It later became part of the School of the Ozarks until it was destroyed by fire. St. Louis schoolchildren ran a successful letter-writing campaign to bring the Liberty Bell to the 1904 World's Fair. When it arrived, there was a parade (one among many at the event) from Lindell to the Pennsylvania building. George Washington's headquarters in Morristown, New Jersey, during the Revolutionary War was reproduced at the fair. Afterward, it was moved to Kirkwood, Missouri, and divided into apartments. The building no longer stands. The Wisconsin building also ended up in Kirkwood as a residence, but it still stands. Perhaps Kirkwood's location on a rail line made it easier to move the buildings there. It should come as no surprise that the Missouri building was the largest and most expensive of the state buildings. One of its virtues was a primitive form of air-conditioning that kept the temperature at seventy degrees. The state hosted one of the fair's most popular guests, Helen Keller, who gave an inspiring speech to the many people who attended.

In addition to education, the 1904 World's Fair offered entertainment. The Pike was the entertainment district. A visitor could buy souvenirs and snacks and stay over at the Inside Inn, one of the most profitable concessions. The Pike was separate from the main exhibits, and although the main fairgrounds closed at night, the Pike remained open and busy. The one issue the concessions had to deal with was that they required payment. So much else at the fair was free.

Probably the most memorable ride at the fair was the Observation Wheel, designed by George Ferris. The Wheel wasn't original to the 1904 World's Fair. It had its debut at the Chicago Fair in 1893. It reached 265 feet above the ground and offered the best aerial view of the fairgrounds and city. There were thirty-six cars that held sixty passengers each. After attempts to sell and move the wheel at the close of the fair failed, it was demolished and sold for scrap. It's still a mystery what happened to the seventy-ton axle, the largest piece of forged steel in the world at the time.

Other favorite rides included the Story of Creation, a spectacular show that included a ride through the story and then a theatrical presentation. There were curiosities, such as contortionists and Jim Key, an educated horse. Hagenbeck's Zoological Paradise and Animal Circus was a favorite. There were animal exhibits and shows featuring bears, monkeys, seals, snakes and elephants. The grand finale of the elephant show had the elephant going down a water slide. Military exhibits replayed the Boer War and naval battles and exhibited Wild West shows. The Scenic Railway, a three-mile roller coaster, grossed $300,000. The Tyrolean Alps, a re-creation of a German village and mountains, had twenty-one buildings and a 25,000-seat restaurant. It grossed over $1 million. The most successful concession, however, was the Inside Inn, a 2,257-room hotel with a 2,500-seat restaurant. It was the fair's biggest moneymaker, grossing $1.5 million. There were other exotic displays and shows, including some that were naughty. One of the visitors commented that if the Pike went any further, it would end up in hell.

With so much happening and so many people, how did fair officials maintain order? That was the job of the Jefferson Guard. These policemen came from across the country and were paid $50/month plus free rooms. Most of the crime at the fair was minor—stolen packages, pickpockets and lost articles and children. However, a garnet necklace was stolen from the German exhibit in the Palace of Agriculture, and $2,500 worth of lace was taken from the Italian exhibit. In the China Pavilion, a woman used her fingernails to pry loose inlays from displayed furniture while talking to attendants! There were some shootings. A waiter trying to get a group to leave a restaurant was shot, and some of the Wild West cowboys settled their disputes with their six-shooters. One of the less serious offenses was "tickling." People would harass others by brushing their skin, in other words, tickling them and then running away.

So, what is left from the fair? The Smithsonian's flight cage was purchased by the City of St. Louis and is still in use at the St. Louis Zoo. The St. Louis Art Museum was the original Palace of Fine Arts at the 1904 World's Fair. And there are fire hydrants, sometimes in odd places, throughout Forest Park that were installed during the event. Many of the buildings that were sold and moved to alternate locations have been torn down or otherwise destroyed in the succeeding years. Keep in mind, the 1904 World's Fair was never meant to be permanent, although it has left an indelible impression on the city as a time when "the world came to St. Louis."

The World's Fair Pavilion
5595 Grand Drive
St. Louis, MO 63112
It is often believed that the World's Fair Pavilion, high atop Government Hill in Forest Park, was part of the 1904 World's Fair. It was not. The pavilion was built with proceeds from the fair in 1909. The fountain and pool were added in the 1930s. In 1998, Forest Park Forever restored the pavilion, and today it is one of the most popular attractions in the park. It is available to rent for special events through the City of St. Louis.

One of the most visited and photographed sites in Forest Park, the World's Fair Pavilion was built after the fair, in 1909. It is available for rental for special events. *Author photo.*

Chapter 8

AFTER THE FAIR

The 1904 World's Fair brought the world to St. Louis, but in the next decade, its leaders decided that the city needed to learn about itself. They planned an enormous Pageant and Masque of Saint Louis to celebrate the sesquicentennial of the founding of the city. On a huge stage, 880 feet wide and 200 feet deep and located at the bottom of Art Hill, more than 7,700 actors appeared in a play that featured depictions of the mound builders of Cahokia, Osage Native Americans, Father Jacques Marquette, Auguste Chouteau, Fort San Carlos, Amos Stoddard accepting Upper Louisiana for the United States, Lewis and Clark, Thomas Hart Benton, the Mexican-American War and nurses caring for the sick and wounded of the Civil War. More than 455,000 persons saw the production over five nights.

Civic leader John Gundlach hailed the pageant as demonstrating "a sustained public spirit for a more humane city." An unexpected profit from the play financed a less-ambitious production in Forest Park of *As You Like It* on a provisional stage in 1916. That location became the site of a permanent outdoor theater, the Municipal Theater of St. Louis, better known as the Muny.

A few animals had been kept in a small zoo in Forest Park, but it became overcrowded by 1912. The city set aside seventy-seven acres for a new zoo and provided for a board to govern it. The park commissioner, tennis champion Dwight F. Davis, opposed the expansion of the zoo in the park, but he was told by Mayor Henry Kiel (who had campaigned for a zoo) that "the people of St. Louis want a zoo awfully bad.…They don't know whether you cut the grass or not—and they don't give a damn. What the people want is a lot of elephants, lions, tigers and monkeys." Those citizens even approved a tax to pay for their desired zoo.

The same decade that saw these civic advances in Forest Park also saw retrograde social policies enacted. By a vote of the people in 1916, St. Louis adopted an ordinance that called for racial segregation of neighborhoods in the city. It prohibited persons of one race from moving to a block where 75 percent of the residents were of another race. Its purpose—hardly disguised during the election campaign—was to keep African Americans confined to certain neighborhoods. Several prominent lawyers offered to file suit against the ordinance for the fee of one dollar. Federal judge D.P. Dyer, a Union veteran, enjoined enforcement of the law as being unconstitutional. However, his order did not prevent the use of private restrictive covenants in deeds prohibiting the sale of property to Blacks. This practice continued until it was declared unconstitutional by the United States Supreme Court in 1948 in a case brought by St. Louis residents J.D. and Ethel Shelley.

St. Louis has always been a baseball town. It had a professional team in the nineteenth century, and when the Milwaukee Brewers moved here in 1902, the city had two major league teams, the Cardinals and the newly renamed Browns. Neither team was particularly successful until after World War I.

In the early 1920s, however, the Browns took off, becoming the most popular team in town. George Sisler led the team, batting .407 with 257 hits in one season (a major league record that stood for eighty-four years) and batting .420 in another. The Browns came close to winning the American League pennant in 1922 but lost by one game to the powerful New York Yankees. The Cardinals had their own hitting star in Rogers Hornsby, who batted .424 in 1924. Finally, in 1926, a St. Louis team won the pennant and defeated the Yankees. But it was the Cardinals, not the Browns. Grover Cleveland Alexander, pitching in relief, reputedly after a hard night on the town, got the Cardinals out of a bases-loaded jam with nobody out. Later in the game, Babe Ruth made the final out of the series when he was thrown out trying to steal second base.

After their World Series win, the Cardinals' fortunes rose and the Browns' plunged. The Cardinals went on to win another ten World Series (to date), led by such stars as Dizzy Dean, Stan Musial, Bob Gibson, Ozzie Smith, Albert Pujols and Yadier Molina. The Browns had no such success and played to as few as 33 fans in one game in 1933 and a historically worst annual attendance of just 80,922 in 1935. They became the punchline in the description of St. Louis as "First in shoes, first in booze and last in the American League."

The two teams shared Sportsman's Park at Grand and Dodier in North St. Louis. In 1944, due to a wartime housing shortage, the managers of the two teams also shared an apartment, but they had to make other arrangements when the Browns and the Cardinals met in the World Series that year. This was the only World Series played in one park until the pandemic of 2020. Although as Stan Musial observed, the fans cheered for the Browns, the Cardinals won. The Browns once again fell into the lower reaches. The team's colorful owner, Bill Veeck, tried to revive fan interest in the team by sending three-foot, seven-inch Eddie Gaedel to bat in one game and having the fans themselves make managerial decisions from the stands in another. But the team's finances were as bad as its performance on the field. It left for Baltimore in 1954.

Anheuser-Busch purchased the Cardinals and owned the team until the 1996 season. The team built a new stadium in downtown St. Louis in 1965 as a part of an extensive urban renewal project that included new hotels, restaurants, office buildings and parking garages. The new stadium was praised by former Yankee and Mets manager Casey Stengel as "holding the heat well." The Cardinals thrived in the 1960s and the 1980s, winning three World Series titles. The team built a new Busch Stadium in 2006, where it has won two more championships. The stadium became the anchor for the Ballpark Village development that has restaurants, the St. Louis Cardinals Hall of Fame, a hotel, an office building and luxury apartments.

St. Louis also played an important role in aviation history in the United States. The first flight here was by Glenn Curtiss in 1909. He later established an aircraft factory that was sold to McDonnell Aircraft after World War II. The world's first parachute jump was made by Colonel Albert Berry over Jefferson Barracks in 1912. Albert Bond Lambert learned to fly from the Wright brothers. In 1920, he leased the land for an airport in Bridgeton. When the lease ran out, he bought the property and sold it to the City of St. Louis in 1928, although it was located in St. Louis County. It is now St. Louis Lambert International Airport.

Charles Lindbergh began his career flying the United States Mail between St. Louis and Chicago. When he decided to attempt the first nonstop solo flight from New York to Paris, a group of St. Louis businessmen led by Lambert financed the trip by closing the deal at the Racquet Club on Kingshighway. In return, Lindbergh named the plane *Spirit of St. Louis*. The original plane is at the National Air and Space Museum. A replica built for the 1957 movie starring Jimmy Stewart hangs in the Grand Hall at the Missouri History Museum. Supposedly, Stewart and Lindbergh each flew it during the filming before it was acquired by the museum.

St. Louis became part of the first rail and air transcontinental service in 1929—its slogan was "Coast to Coast in 48 Hours"—established by Transcontinental Air Transport, a predecessor to Trans World Airlines. By the 1990s, Lambert Airport was a hub for TWA's national and international flights, but the airline's frequent bankruptcies and ultimate acquisition by American Airlines spelled an end to its long history.

During World War II, the airport expanded to meet military needs. On August 2, 1943, a glider carrying the mayor, six other dignitaries and two crew members crashed on a demonstration flight, killing everyone on board and evoking memories of an 1855 railroad accident. In that incident, a train full of St. Louis VIPs fell into the Gasconade River, killing thirty-one passengers and injuring many others, including the mayor of St. Louis.

In the postwar era, McDonnell Aircraft built the first jet fighters to be carried on aircraft carriers, as well as other stalwart military aircraft and commercial airliners. The company also built Mercury and Gemini space capsules. McDonnell Douglas merged with the Douglas Aircraft Company in 1967 and with the Boeing Aircraft Company in 1997. The James S. McDonnell Prologue Room at Boeing's St. Lous headquarters has, among other exhibits, two full-size examples of Mercury and Gemini capsules.

Luther Ely Smith, a St. Louis lawyer, floated the idea for a riverfront memorial to Westward Expansion in 1933 with hopes that the project would also revitalize the city. After a contentious election approving the idea, President Franklin Roosevelt signed an Executive Order creating the Jefferson National Expansion Memorial (now called the Gateway Arch National Park) in 1935. As Smith had originally hoped, the St. Louis riverfront was selected as the site. Forty city blocks were purchased and cleared, remaining that way for a number of years due to World War II. In 1947, a competition was held for a design for the memorial. It was won by Finnish American architect Eero Saarinen. Today, the Gateway Arch is instantly recognizable around the world as the symbol of St. Louis.

In the years after World War I, business leaders shepherded through a series of bond issues for numerous improvements to the city. One of these was for the clearance of several blocks to allow for the construction of a memorial to men and women who died in the service of their country during World War I. It took nearly fourteen years, but in 1936, President Franklin Roosevelt dedicated the Soldiers Memorial Military Museum. The building was completed in 1938. A cenotaph in the loggia has the names of 1,075 St. Louisans who died during that war. The Court of Honor across Chestnut Street was created in the 1940s to add the names of St. Louisans who died in World War II. Later, the names of those who fell in the Korean and Vietnam Wars were added. In 2019, the museum included the names of all service personnel in the entire St. Louis region who have died on active duty since the Vietnam War. Although owned by the City of St. Louis, the recently renovated museum is now operated by the Missouri Historical Society.

St. Louis has many other cultural institutions, both old and new. They include the following: the National Museum of Transportation (opened in 1944); the St. Louis Cardinals Hall of Fame Museum (reopened in 2014); Laumeier Sculpture Park (1976); the St. Louis Kaplan Feldman Holocaust Museum (1995); the Griot Museum of Black History and Culture (formerly the Black World History Wax Museum) (1997); and the National Blues Museum (2016).

St. Louis Art Museum

1 Fine Arts Drive
St. Louis, MO 63110

Today's St. Louis Art Museum traces its lineage to the St. Louis School and Museum of Fine Arts, founded in 1879 and located downtown. It operated in conjunction with Washington University but was a separate institution.

In 1904, Cass Gilbert designed the Palace of Fine Arts for the 1904 World's Fair, the only permanent building at the fairgrounds. Museums from around the world were sending artworks to be displayed at the fair and didn't want to risk placing them in temporary buildings subject to fire.

Today, the collection spans the globe from antiquity to the present and features Egyptian mummies, Native American art, the world's largest collection by German painter Max Beckmann and a constantly changing array of special exhibits.

Admission to the museum is always free, although there may be a charge for special exhibits.

The statue of Louis IX of France, the namesake of the city, stands outside the St. Louis Art Museum at the top of Art Hill. The statue originally appeared during the St. Louis World's Fair in plaster, sculpted by Charles Henry Niehaus. During the fair, it stood near the north entrance, approximately where the Missouri History Museum is today. After the fair, the Louisiana Purchase Exposition Company had the statue cast in bronze and presented it as a gift

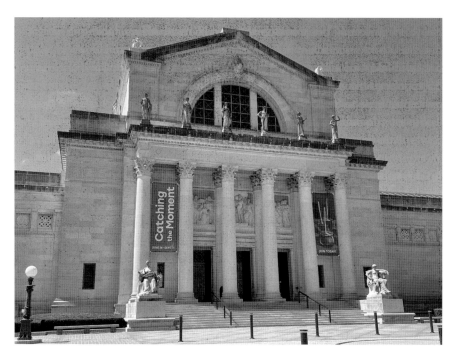

Above: The main structure of the St. Louis Art Museum has changed little since the 1904 World's Fair, although there have been additions not visible in this photo. *Author photo*.

Left: The official name of the statue in front of the St. Louis Art Museum is *Apotheosis of St. Louis*. Before the Gateway Arch, this statue was often used as a symbol of the city. *Author photo*.

to the City of St. Louis. For many years, Louis IX, atop his horse and holding his sword high, was the symbol of the city. Many businesses, including the St. Louis Browns baseball team, incorporated the statue into their logos. The statue's formal name is *Apotheosis of St. Louis*.

The Cathedral Basilica of St. Louis

4431 Lindell Boulevard
St. Louis, MO 63108

By the late nineteenth century, the population of St. Louis had reached a level that Archbishop John J. Kain perceived that a new cathedral was necessary. During his tenure, the archdiocese purchased land, but plans were delayed after St. Louis suffered a devastating tornado and Kain fell ill. His successor, Archbishop John J. Glennon, announced the building of the new cathedral in 1905. Cost was estimated at $1 million, an unheard-of sum for the day. Ground-breaking occurred on May 1, 1907, and construction continued for the next eighty years.

The first Mass was celebrated on October 18, 1914, in a not-yet-completed building. The first wedding was celebrated two days later. The bride's parents donated the money for the High Altar.

The cathedral was finally consecrated on June 29, 1926, the centennial of the creation of the Diocese of St. Louis. Fifty-nine archbishops and priests attended the ceremony, witnessed by over one hundred thousand people, who lined Lindell Boulevard to view the procession of the Blessed Sacrament.

The cathedral is known for its mosaics. Installation began in 1912 and was completed in 1988. There are estimated to be 41.5 million pieces of glass in seven thousand colors.

In 1997, Pope John Paul II designated the cathedral a basilica. He further honored the Cathedral Basilica of St. Louis when he visited in January 1999. Today, his tintinnabulum (bell) and ombrellino (umbrella) remain on either side of the High Altar as a reminder of its special status.

The Holy Spirit Adoration Sisters (better known as the "Pink Sisters" because of the color of their habit) pray around the clock at their sequestered convent in St. Louis. Before the pope's visit, they sent up their prayers for good weather. On John Paul II's first day in St. Louis (in January), it was fifty-six degrees. The second day was even more pleasant, reaching sixty-eight degrees. The sisters credited a higher power. While in St. Louis, the pope met with then President Bill Clinton, St. Louis's legendary Stan Musial and civil rights icon Rosa Parks.

The New Cathedral, or Cathedral Basilica of St. Louis, is adorned with beautiful mosaics. *St. Louis Landmarks.*

The cathedral also features a museum telling the story of the mosaics. In addition, it features the original Kilgan organ, the throne used by Pope John Paul II on his historic visit and historic vestments. The cathedral crypt holds the remains of Archbishop John May and Cardinals Glennon, Joseph Ritter and John Carberry.

Daily Masses are celebrated, and tours may be arranged. Archives containing records, artifacts, photos and memorabilia of the Cathedral Basilica of St. Louis are available by appointment.

The Muny

1 Theatre Drive
St. Louis, MO 63112

The St. Louis Municipal Opera became the first outdoor theater in a major U.S. city in 1916. It was the 300th anniversary of Shakespeare's death, and *As You Like It* was the first performance. Financing came from the profits generated by an outdoor staging of Pageant and Masque of Saint Louis put on at the foot of Forest Park's Art Hill to celebrate the 150th birthday of the city. The park commissioner chose the location for *As You Like It*, between two large oak trees on a cleared hillside. This provided a level stage for the theater. As has happened many times in Muny history, opening night was rained out. Attendance averaged eight thousand theatergoers each night.

The next year, the Advertising Club's annual convention was to be held in St. Louis. Guy Golterman, a member of the club, convinced the park commissioner that a performance of *Aida* in the open air of Forest Park would be excellent entertainment for the club. He also sweetened the deal with an offer of $6,000 to make it happen. The commissioner matched the $6,000 and, along with additional donations, erected a concrete amphitheater to house the performance. *Aida* opened and, as you may suspect, was rained on.

When St. Louis mayor Henry Kiel was approached with the idea that the outdoor stage be used to present theater all summer, he was hesitant. But with much cajoling by theater supporters, he finally agreed that the city stage could be used, but the theater would be run by private individuals. The producers also agreed that only light opera not being shown anywhere else would be presented. The theater was promoted as musical education, and soon St. Louisans were bragging that they had more knowledge of and exposure to light opera than anyplace else in the United States.

From the beginning, the Muny influenced future performers. Christian Ludoff Ebsen from Belleville, Illinois, attended the 1919 opening night. Christian is better known as Buddy Ebsen, of Broadway, movie and television fame. In 1926, five-time Academy Award nominee Irene Dunn debuted at the Muny. When Charles Lindbergh returned to St. Louis after his famous New York–Paris flight (financed by St. Louisans) in 1927, he ended a three-day visit with a trip to the Muny. Archie Leach debuted at the Muny in 1931 in *The Street Singer* before he changed his name to Cary Grant. Mary Wickes, Phyllis Diller, Red Skelton, Debbie Reynolds, Ethel Merman, Pearl Bailey, Bob Hope, Jerry Orbach, Lauren Bacall, John Travolta, Carol Channing, Angela Lansbury, Yul Brynner, Agnes Morehead and Bernadette Peters are just a sampling of the stars who have appeared on the Muny stage.

By the late 1920s, opera was no longer as popular with Muny audiences. A second outdoor theater had opened in University City, hosting musical comedy, often with the original Broadway stars. The summer of 1930 became a turning point. Milton Schubert was brought on board to bring the Muny up to date. He improved the lighting and sound, added a revolving stage and brought in New York costumers, choreographers and directors to stage more modern musicals.

There are many stories of stars and stage that are part of Muny lore. For example, it was a tradition to buy a trunk in St. Louis at a famous luggage maker on Washington Avenue for Muny actors, and Archie Leach (Cary Grant) followed that tradition, having his monogrammed with "A.L." It even included a special compartment for a top hat. At the end of the season, he left the trunk behind with a fellow actor, as Leach rushed off to take on a part in a Broadway show. That actor befriended St. Louis resident and actor Mary Wickes. Mary ended up with the trunk and loved it, carrying it to many performances in theaters far and wide. Alas, Archie never reclaimed his property.

Broadway star Ken Page performed on the Muny stage, reprising his roles as Old Deuteronomy in *Cats*, Ken in *Ain't Misbehavin'* and more. Ken tried out for the Muny before he "made it" on Broadway and was turned away twice before securing a place in the singing chorus.

Ann Miller was a favorite on the stage. In 1972, she was performing in Cole Porter's *Anything Goes* when a piece of equipment grazed her head. Fifteen physicians responded to a call to the audience for medical assistance. Miller was unable to continue in the performance, and her understudy, a local girl studying at Webster University, took over the role with only a few hours' notice.

For many years, the Muny avoided what was referred to as "star driven" shows, insisting that the show itself was the star. However, in the 1970s, it changed direction, inviting summer tours with big name stars to the stage (see above for some of the stars who appeared).

In the 1980s, the Muny stretched its wings and leased the stage at the Fox Theatre for a minimum of twelve weeks between September and May. The lease was for ten years and was the first time the Muny had moved to an indoor venue.

Another perk of having the Muny in St. Louis was the training it provided young hopefuls for the stage. Some stayed in St. Louis, continuing to be appear in professional productions without having to leave the city. Others left and went forward, well trained for their career.

For years, the Muny stage was framed by two burr oaks, the original trees chosen to frame the first Muny performance. In 2002, one of those trees, sadly, had to come down.

The Muny has a tradition of staging the musicals with twists unavailable in other venues. For example, during *South Pacific*, a plane flies overhead indicating Lieutenant Joe Cable's arrival—not something that can be done inside.

Another Muny tradition that has been practiced since the beginning is a section of free seats always available to showgoers.

St. Louis Zoo

1 Government Drive
St. Louis, MO 63110

The St. Louis Zoo is one of the top zoos in the country, and it's free to visit every day.

The Smithsonian Institution built a bird cage for $17,500 for the 1904 World's Fair, and it proved to be very popular with fair guests. After the fair, citizens decided it would be beneficial to keep the walk-through cage in the city. Rather than dismantle it and send it back to Washington, D.C., the Smithsonian sold it to the city for just $3,500, and it became the cornerstone of the St. Louis Zoo. The birds were not part of the purchase, but the zoo added Mandarin ducks, Canada geese and owls as a beginning.

The bird cage wasn't the only reason the St. Louis Zoological Society came into being in 1910. City fathers believed a zoo would make St. Louis a better place for residents and visitors alike. In the words of the zoo's first director, George Vierheller, "There are two things a lively city needs—a good zoo and a good baseball team."

There was still controversy brewing, mostly over the location of the new zoo. Forest Park was the logical choice, but the city's park commissioners were worried that adding a zoo would ruin the natural beauty of the park. The proponents of the Forest Park location won after three years of wrangling. Seventy acres were set aside for the zoo.

From the beginning, the mission of the St. Louis Zoo exceeded a desire to provide entertainment for visitors. Research, providing protection to wildlife and encouraging public interest in the animals were and still are goals the zoo seeks to fulfill.

The first elephant came to the zoo in 1916. Schoolchildren donated to a penny drive to purchase Miss Jim (named after the president of the school board), an Asian elephant and former circus performer. She was a popular attraction for over thirty years.

In 1921, as part of its mission to exhibit animals under favorable conditions, the zoo added the Bear Pits. They have become a model of natural habitat for zoos everywhere. The bluffs of the pits were and are concrete, created from molds of rock formations along the Mississippi River. A moat encloses the pits. Over the years, the zoo has added more natural habitats to exhibits, including River's Edge for rhinoceros and hippopotami, Penguin and Puffin Coast, Stingrays Caribbean Cove, Cypress Swamp in the 1904 Flight Cage, Sea Lion Sound, Big Cat Country, the Insectarium and the Jungle of the Apes.

This sculpture welcomes visitors to the St. Louis Zoo. It is one of many sculptures that grace the grounds, along with their live counterparts. *Author photo.*

One of the most beloved animals at of all time was Phil the Gorilla, who came to the zoo in 1941. He was only twenty-six pounds when he arrived. Phil was very playful, splashing onlookers, swinging on pipes and throwing tires at the bars of his cage toward the crowd. In 1954, Phil was featured in *Life* magazine. When he died in 1958, his obituary ran on the front page of local papers.

St. Louis Zoo has always had stellar directors, but three stand out. The first director of the zoo, George Vierheller, was a showman. He created animal shows, turning the participating "stars" into local celebrities. They were featured in newsreels, and *Life* called the St. Louis Zoo "the most entertaining [zoo] in the U.S."

Marlin Perkins was the second full-time director of the St. Louis Zoo. He was hired as a groundskeeper but soon was put in charge of the zoo's six reptiles. During his eleven-year tenure as curator of reptiles, he created a home for them and increased the collection. When he returned to the zoo as director in 1962, he had built a national reputation, based partly on his television programs, most notably *Mutual of Omaha's Wild Kingdom*. He had a lifelong interest in ecology and conservation that became an even more integral part of the work of the St. Louis Zoo.

The showmanship continued with Charlie Hoessle, named director in 1982 after filling a number of jobs and creating the Education Department. Hoessle's special interest was reptiles. Hoessle was born and raised in St. Louis, and he had his own exotic animal business before coming to work at the zoo. He continued the showmanship of prior directors by hosting the local television *St. Louis Zoo Show*. Hoessle phased out the animal shows, preferring to have visitors view animals doing what animals naturally do rather than show them doing tricks and dressed up in costumes, which has no connection to the life of the animal. He was in charge when many of the natural habitats were developed. Hoessle retired in 2002 and was named director emeritus.

Today, the St. Louis Zoo is the home of more than fourteen thousand animals representing nearly five hundred species. It welcomes more visitors than any other St. Louis attraction.

Shelley House

4600 Labadie
St. Louis, MO 63115

This modest, two-story home was the centerpiece of a decision by the United States Supreme Court that was one of the first blows against segregation in the long battle to enforce the rights of African Americans under the Fourteenth Amendment. J.D. Shelley and his wife, Ethel, purchased this home in 1945. Neighbors sued to enforce a covenant that purported to prohibit the sale of any home in the area to persons other than Caucasians. When the case reached the Supreme Court, the Shelleys' lawyer, George Vaughn, concluded his argument by saying that the "Negro knocks at America's door," rapping his knuckles loudly on the podium. The sound reverberated throughout the silent courtroom. "Let me come in and sit by the fire. I helped build the house." In 1948, the court ruled that enforcement of the racially restrictive covenant was a violation of the equal protection of the law.

The Shelley House is part of the National African American Civil Rights Network. It is in private hands.

Gateway Arch National Park

11 North Fourth Street
St. Louis, MO 63102

There is nothing that evokes St. Louis as vividly as the Gateway Arch. A project that was begun in 1935 finally came to fruition in 1965, when the ten-ton keystone piece was placed at the highest point in the structure.

The arch design was one of three firsts in the history of engineering on the riverfront. The first was the Eads Bridge, the first bridge to use a tubular steel arch structure. Eads Bridge, built in 1874, is the oldest span over the Mississippi River and forms the northern edge of the Gateway Arch Park. The second forms the southern boundary and is also a bridge. This one was the first to use an orthotropic design, which refers to the use of steel decking. And the third is the engineering marvel of the Gateway Arch, a design Eero Saarinen borrowed from the Eads Bridge.

Saarinen's major concern "was to create a monument which would have lasting significance and would be a landmark of our time." Unfortunately, he did not live to see his work completed. Saarinen died in 1961 after surgery for a brain tumor.

The Gateway Arch is the tallest monument in the United States measuring 630 feet tall. It is sixty-three stories high and constructed of forty-three thousand tons of concrete and steel. A tram takes visitors to the top viewing area, where it's possible to see (on a clear day) thirty miles east and west.

The Gateway Arch and the related park celebrate westward expansion and St. Louis's role in it. It also spotlights 201 years of history (1767–1965) of Native Americans, pioneers, explorers and everyone with a dream and a vision. Underneath the Gateway Arch is a museum that covers the history of St. Louis and westward expansion in six "story galleries." The first covers colonial St. Louis, featuring indigenous and Creole culture before the Louisiana Purchase. At the time, St. Louis was a hub for fur trade and a city bustling with Native Americans, French and Spanish officials and entrepreneurs looking to make their fortunes. And what drew these people? Location, location,

The Gateway Arch, the symbol of St. Louis, is known around the world. *National Park Service.*

location. The city was near the confluence of two major rivers, the Missouri and the Mississippi, major highways of the day.

Jefferson's Vision, featuring the Lewis and Clark expedition, is featured next. Jefferson wanted the United States to come out on top of an ongoing struggle for control of land in North America, and this was his important step.

The mid-1800s and America's belief in Manifest Destiny, or America's God-given right to expand, is the next story presented. Wars and treaties paved the way west, although conflict still existed over whom the land belonged to.

Steamboats and the riverboat era had a broad influence on St. Louis and westward expansion. The arrival of the first steamboat in St. Louis made way for the Missouri River becoming the Gateway to the West. The Port of St. Louis was important in the distribution of goods to the West.

The late 1840s brought manufacturing to the city and opened a New Frontier. By the 1870s, St. Louis was a top industrial city. This story investigates how industry changed the city. This section of the museum also takes a look at the myth of the West versus its reality.

And finally, visitors are invited to take a look into Building the Arch. No one had ever built anything like it before.

A tram ride takes guests to the top of the Gateway Arch for out-of-this-world views of the city and the river. After seeing it from above, visitors can see the remainder of the park. Luther Ely Smith Square, named after the St. Louisan who first proposed a riverfront memorial to Thomas Jefferson and Westward Expansion, is a green space where visitors can relax and enjoy the ground-level views. It leads from the Arch's entrance to one of the oldest buildings still standing in St. Louis, the Old Courthouse. Across the street is Kiener Plaza, named for Harry Kiener, a track-and-field participant in the 1904 Olympics who became a successful businessman and philanthropist. It stretches to the Civil Courts Building and provides more green space to relax as well as a place to participate in local events.

Soldiers Memorial Military Museum

1315 Chestnut Street
St. Louis, MO 63103

The Soldiers Memorial Military Museum has permanent exhibits about all branches of the military from the Revolutionary War to the present day on the first floor. The second floor has meeting rooms used for frequent programs relating to America's military. The basement houses special exhibits. Of note are four sculptures on the steps of the memorial designed and produced by Walker Hancock, a well-known artist born in St. Louis. These are *Courage*, *Loyalty*, *Vision* and *Sacrifice*. The latter statue features a woman holding a baby. It caused considerable controversy when it was proposed. The city objected to the extra $1,000 it cost when Hancock revised his design. After an embarrassing public relations debacle, Hancock convinced the city that the infant was critical to the composition and symbolism of sacrifice, and it agreed to pay the bill.

Hancock later received significant commissions for work on other buildings, such as the Washington National Cathedral and the United States Supreme Court. During World War II, he served as one of the "Monuments Men," recovering art stolen by the Nazis.

Soldiers Memorial is owned by the City of St. Louis and operated as an arm of the Missouri History Museum. *Author photo.*

The Fabulous Fox Theatre

527 North Grand Boulevard
St. Louis, MO 63103

From the time it opened until the present day, the Fox Theatre has featured the best in entertainment in midtown St. Louis. It has offered and continues to offer movies, Broadway shows, music concerts and an occasional taste of Vegas.

William Fox was a visionary in the motion-picture industry. He bought his first nickelodeon in 1904 and, once moving pictures caught on, expanded into a chain of theaters in the 1920s. After suing and prevailing in a court proceeding against Thomas Edison's Motion Pictures Patent Company, Fox started his own production company and made stars of Tom Mix and Theda Bara. He brought sound on tape to the United States from abroad and pioneered wide screens. After being forced out of his company and serving a prison term for bribing a judge during his bankruptcy proceeding in 1931, Fox was no longer welcome in Hollywood.

However, before being blacklisted, in 1927, he brought the opulent Fox Theatre to St. Louis. Movie theaters were the palaces of the time, and those C. Howard Crane designed were known for ornate designs and excellent

An opulent movie theater in its early days, the Fox Theatre today is a place to see Broadway at its finest. *St. Louis Landmarks.*

acoustics. The Fox design was described as Siamese Byzantine, a combination of Moorish, Far Eastern, Egyptian, Babylonian and Indian from a variety of periods. The opulent lobby was reminiscent of an ancient Indian religious building. It had rows of flanking columns in the large lobby, and its terrazzo floors were covered with imported carpets. Crimson and gold were the primary colors used in the building. Taking almost two years to build at a cost of $5 million, the Fox opened to grand acclaim.

The Fabulous Fox has shared its stage with movies and stars throughout the years. It was the site of movie premieres for *St. Louis Blues* starring Nat King Cole (1939), *The Spirit of St. Louis* (1957) and *The*

Trouble with Angels (1966), among others. In the 1930s, Ziegfeld Follies star Ruth Etting appeared in person, and Paul Whiteman placed twenty-one pianos throughout the theater to play "Rhapsody in Blue." In 1940, Bob Hope came to the stage with the Jerry Colonna Radio Troupe and sold eighty thousand tickets in one week.

From 1959 to 1978, the Fox was one of three movie palaces located in proximity, and the competition was fierce. Despite a valiant try by the owners to keep the theater alive, the doors closed in 1978.

In 1981, Fox Associates bought the property, and Mary Strauss directed the restoration. After careful study, Strauss decided to stay as close as possible to the original design and, in time, turned the Fox Theatre into the Fabulous Fox Theatre. New carpet kept the original pattern, the chandelier in the auditorium was redone and every one of the 4,500 seats was removed, restored and reinstalled.

The Fabulous Fox Theatre reopened in September 1982 as a performing arts center, with everything updated to provide for contemporary entertainment. In 1994–95, the stage was enlarged to accommodate Broadway touring shows. The lobby was restored in 2000, including new paint, faux marble columns and restoration of the ceiling mural. A new sign was installed in 2008, replicating the original.

National Museum of Transportation
2933 Barrett Station Road
St. Louis, MO 63122

The National Museum of Transportation was founded in 1944. It is located on the former Missouri Pacific Railroad where the mainline ran through the West Barrett's Tunnel, one of the first tunnels west of the Mississippi River. The museum is now in the National Register of Historic Places.

On display are dozens of steam and diesel locomotives, including such historic ones as the Union Pacific Big Boy (132 feet long and weighing 1.2 million pounds); the Electro-Motive Division FT 103, an innovative freight diesel locomotive (and a National Engineering Landmark) whose success led to the replacement of steam locomotives on the nation's railroads; and the Bellefontaine Mule Car, the first artifact acquired by the museum. Also on the property are the H.T. POTT towboat and C-47 Army transport plane (the military version of the DC-3). Automobile enthusiasts can see Bobby Darin's Dream Car, hand-built over seven years at a cost of $93,000 (more than $1 million today).

The museum has a transportation research library, a large gift shop, an interactive transportation-themed play and educational area for young children, a miniature train and a full-sized trolley.

St. Louis Cardinals Baseball Hall of Fame and Museum

700 Clark Avenue (Ballpark Village)
St. Louis, MO 63102

The St. Louis Cardinals are one of the most historic and successful major league franchises. The museum has over fifteen thousand artifacts and eighty thousand photographs, second only to the National Baseball Hall of Fame in its holdings. The museum's seven galleries take you on a chronological journey through the history of the team. The exhibits include one-of-a-kind stadium models that showcase each home of the Redbirds, from Sportsman's Park to the current Busch Stadium, and an opportunity to make your own call of some of the Cardinals' most memorable moments in "The Broadcast Booth."

Laumeier Sculpture Park

12580 Rott Road
St. Louis, MO 63127

In 1976, Matilda Laumeier bequeathed 72 acres to St. Louis County for an outdoor sculpture park. Artist Ernest Trova donated forty of his works, worth $1 million. St. Louis County Parks officially took over the park in 1977. Today, it has 105 acres and over seventy large-scale outdoor sculptures. Free and open daily, Laumeier serves three hundred thousand visitors of all ages each year through sculpture conservation, education programs, temporary exhibitions and public events.

St. Louis Kaplan Feldman Holocaust Museum

12 Millstone Campus Drive
St. Louis, MO 63146

The St. Louis Kaplan Feldman Holocaust Museum opened in 1995 in honor of the survivors and in memory of the victims. The museum is dedicated to preserving the legacy of the Holocaust, educating about the causes and teaching how what happened during that time relates to the present day. The lessons promote rejecting hatred while encouraging understanding and inspiring change.

Survivors of the Holocaust are the heart of the museum. They have donated family photos, documents and heirlooms. By their presence and the presence of these precious objects, the experience of visitors becomes personal. The survivors share their stories in docent-led tours of the museum and find it especially important to talk to students. As the number of survivors fades, their relatives continue to share the important stories of loved ones.

The band of survivors who came to St. Louis felt it important to make sure the Holocaust was never forgotten. The museum is a result of their work.

The museum is undergoing renovation and expansion to keep up with not only the Holocaust but also recent events such as the Rwanda genocide, white supremacist murders and aggression toward the LGBTQ+ community.

The first stop in the museum is an area that shows the diversity of individuals and their lives before the tragedy of the Holocaust. It features St. Louis survivors and relatives of St. Louis residents who died. Visitors move into an exhibit featuring Jewish life in Europe before the Holocaust and then the rise of Nazism. Exhibits of what happened in the early years of World War II, the ghettos, the camps and the resistance, follow, leading to the Final Solution and transport to the East. Liberation and rescue are illustrated, along with the Nuremburg Trials. Finally, Jewish life after the Holocaust includes rebuilding, displaced person camps, Israel, the United States and attempts to return home.

The Oral History Project is an important aspect of the museum's mission. A digital library of survivor stories as well as stories of those who aided or were in some way touched by the Holocaust are available.

Griot Museum of Black History and Culture

2505 St. Louis Avenue
St. Louis, MO 63106

The Griot Museum of Black History and Culture opened in 1997 as the Black World History Wax Museum. It changed its name in 2009 but still features life-size wax figures of such important persons as Josephine Baker, Dred and Harriet Scott, Elizabeth Keckley, William Wells Brown, James Milton Turner, Dr. Martin Luther King Jr. and Miles Davis. The museum hosts an extensive assortment of artifacts, art and memorabilia that illustrate the contribution of Black persons to the country's development. It has an authentic slave cabin from a plantation in Jonesburg, Missouri. There is also a scale model of a section of a ship of the type used in the transatlantic slave trade. In addition to its permanent collection, the Griot also hosts traveling local and national arts and humanities exhibits and sponsors community education projects, gallery talks and cultural celebrations.

The museum's name comes from the griot, a societal leader in some West African countries who records and passes on important events such as births, deaths, marriages and cultural traditions. A historian, storyteller, praise singer, poet and/or musician, the griot shares stories through a variety of formats.

National Blues Museum

615 Washington Avenue
St. Louis, MO 63101

Located in a renovated historic building in downtown St. Louis, the National Blues Museum opened in 2016 to provide a history of the many and varied styles and sources of blues music from different periods and different places. Its website describes a large part of its mission as the delivery of educational resources "to provide an enhanced museum experience for students and educators, facilitate the creation of classroom resources and traveling exhibits to demonstrate the power of music and America's rich musical heritage, engage children and families to encourage musical appreciation and expression, increase access to music programs in underprivileged communities, address race, diversity and culture through the Blues, serve as a center for education and collaboration and creating partnerships with other museums and educators." The museum hosts frequent live performances.

Frank Lloyd Wright Homes in St. Louis

Russell Kraus House
120 North Ballas Road
St. Louis, MO 63122

Theodore A. Pappas House
865 Mason Ridge Road
Town and Country, MO 63017

Frank Lloyd Wright is one of the preeminent architects in the United States. His first brush with St. Louis was when he worked with Louis Sullivan on the Wainwright Building downtown. At the age of twenty-two, he started his own architecture firm in Oak Park, Illinois, and created Prairie Style architecture, reflective of the Midwest landscape with horizontal lines, earth tones and a connection between inside and outside. He later created Usonian homes meant for middle-income families. He believed everyone should have access to beautiful architecture. Usonian homes used geometric modules and eliminated basements, attics and garages as a cost-saving measure.

Russell Kraus was a nationally known St. Louis artist who worked in a variety of media, mainly stained glass and mosaic, but also textile, jewelry, sculpture and painting. While working on a WPA art project, he met Ruth Goetz, an attorney, and they married in 1949.

When Kraus read about Usonian homes in *House Beautiful* magazine, he wrote to Wright, asking him to design a home for him and his wife. The architect answered him five days later: "You should have the nice little house. Condense your needs...and we will make you a plan."

Once Wright agreed and came up with a design, the Krauses hired a construction foreman but oversaw the project themselves. The geometric design of the Kraus House is based on an equilateral parallelogram with a complex floor plan of intersecting parallelograms. The home features an open living area with concrete floors. There is a wall of glass doors to make the outdoors part of the home. The structure uses brick, concrete and glass to achieve the goals of the design. Kraus's stained glass and mosaic work are also incorporated into the home. A specially designed studio provided the artist with a workspace for his commercial art business. The house is located on ten and a half wooded acres and is 1,900 square feet. It was the first Frank Lloyd Wright home in St. Louis and one of only five in Missouri.

Ruth and Russell Kraus moved into the home in 1956, but the furniture, also designed by Wright, took more time to complete. Ruth wrote to Wright about the house: "We love our house, Mr. Wright. Love it passionately and intensely. To us, it is not inanimate brick, mortar, steel, and wood. To us it is a personality. A thing that lives and breathes."

Ruth died in 1992. Russell continued to live in the house until 2001, when he sold the property to the Frank Lloyd Wright House in Ebsworth Park, which in turn promptly deeded the home to St. Louis County. It is now a public park and museum. The Frank Lloyd Wright House in Ebsworth Park organization still manages the property and has renovated the house. It is open for tours by appointment.

The second Frank Lloyd Wright home in St. Louis County is the Theodore A. Pappas House, built by the Pappas family in 1960–64. It is the second-largest of what is termed the Usonian Automatic home, designed to be a house built by the owner as a do-it-yourself project. These homes are a series of plain concrete blocks stacked on top of and next to one another with no

Ruth and Russell Kraus are the only residents to live in their Frank Lloyd Wright–designed home, now a county park located in Kirkwood, Missouri. *Photo courtesy of David Charles.*

mortar. There are hollows within the blocks for steel rods inserted vertically and horizontally, then filled with mortar after. The concrete used for the blocks is pre-tinted because Wright believed that the color should be in the block, not applied to its surface. The house has four bedrooms and two bathrooms and is located on 3.36 wooded acres.

The house is currently owned by the Frank Lloyd Wright Revival Initiative, an organization whose goal is to preserve all of Wright's remaining buildings. Limited tours are available.

Chapter 9

ST. LOUIS NEIGHBORHOODS

There are seventy-nine official neighborhoods in the City of St. Louis. Many of these include structures of historic interest. They include the following:

Benton Park

Benton Park neighborhood is named for the park located there. Benton is the second-oldest park in St. Louis and is named after U.S. senator Thomas Hart Benton. The Chatillon-DeMenil House and the Lemp Mansion are located in this neighborhood.

Bevo Mill

This neighborhood is named for and surrounds a city landmark built by August Busch Sr. in 1917, the Bevo Mill. The beer garden is located on Gravois Road halfway between the brewery and the Busch family home at Grant's Farm. Mr. Busch often stopped at the mill on his way home from work to imbibe a glass of his favorite beverage, wine. The beer garden was actually part of a carefully planned propaganda campaign on the part of Anheuser-Busch to create an image in people's minds that beer wasn't the evil liquid about to be banned by Prohibition but part and parcel of a normal family life.

Carondelet

The area now known as Carondelet neighborhood was originally a separate town from St. Louis, settled by French immigrants from Illinois. It was annexed by

Bevo Mill, built by August Busch Sr., is still a St. Louis landmark. *Missouri Historical Society.*

Des Peres School was the site of the first kindergarten in the United States, founded by Susan Blow. Today, it is the home of the Carondelet Historical Society. *St. Louis Landmarks.*

St. Louis in 1870. The first public kindergarten in the United States was founded in the Des Peres School by Susan Blow. It became a model for kindergartens around the country. The school building is now the home of the Carondelet Historical Society.

Central West End

Streets in this neighborhood in the center of the city are named after those who acquired land after the Louisiana Purchase. The area includes Forest Park and the New Cathedral.

Clayton/Tamm (Dogtown)

The Clayton/Tamm neighborhood is named after the two major streets that cross at its center. It is known for Turtle Park, a small park near the zoo that features sculptures of turtles, perfect for children to climb on. The area was settled by Irish immigrants, and that heritage is highlighted in the annual St. Patrick's Day Parade, sponsored by the Ancient Order of Hibernians. The Dogtown name probably derives from a group of Irish miners who worked in the area that became known as Forest Park, mining clay until the park designation took away their jobs. While waiting to find new work, they lived in shacks in the Clayton/Tamm area, and many used dogs to guard their property.

Columbus Square

Once predominantly Irish, this area was known as the "Kerry Patch." It is the location of the Shrine of St. Joseph, the site of the only Vatican-authenticated miracle in the Midwest.

Grand Center

Many of St. Louis's arts venues are located in this neighborhood, including Powell Symphony Hall, the Fox Theatre, Sheldon Concert Hall, art galleries and museum.

Downtown

Downtown is the central business district of the city. There are sports venues such as Busch Stadium, which houses the St. Louis Cardinals baseball team, and many historic sites, including the Eugene Field House, the Old Courthouse, the Wainwright Building, Eads Bridge and more.

Lafayette Square, the home of St. Louis's rich and powerful, was destroyed by a tornado. Its residents moved farther west. The neighborhood was revived in the 1970s, and many of the beautiful Victorian homes were rehabbed. *Missouri History Museum.*

The Hill

The Hill is famous for its Italian heritage and as the birthplace of toasted ravioli and baseball great Yogi Berra. There are many Italian restaurants, bakeries and groceries to explore.

Lafayette Square

Originally part of the St. Louis Commons, the neighborhood is named after Lafayette Park, which sits at its center. Lafayette Park is the oldest park in St. Louis and the oldest park west of the Mississippi River. The area, at the time the location of many lovely homes, was devastated in the tornado of 1896 and didn't really come back until the 1960s. It was named the city's first historic district in 1972.

Shaw

Henry Shaw, the man behind the Missouri Botanical Garden, was influential in developing the neighborhood around what was at the time his home. The

141

restrictions on the houses built resulted in creating a neighborhood with uniform architecture. Shaw Place was developed by Henry Shaw as rental property to provide an income for an endowment for his garden project. Trustees of the Garden sold the homes in 1915.

Chapter 10

LOCAL HISTORICAL SOCIETIES IN THE ST. LOUIS METRO AREA

T here are more than two hundred historical societies in the St. Louis area that deal with history on a local level. These organizations are often housed in historic homes or structures. They can be particularly helpful when doing genealogical research. Some of the historical societies are associated with city government; others are independent societies. The following are just a few.

AFFTON HISTORICAL SOCIETY
Oakland House
7801 Genesta Street
St. Louis, MO 63123
www.Oaklandhouse.org

BEVO AREA HISTORICAL SOCIETY
4728 Adkins Avenue
Saint Louis, MO 63116

CARONDELET HISTORICAL SOCIETY
Old Des Peres School/Carondelet Historical Museum
6303 Michigan Avenue
St. Louis, MO 63111
www.carondelethistory.org

Civil War Roundtable of St. Louis
www.civilwarstlmo.org

Clayton Missouri Historical Society
2 Mark Twain Circle
Clayton, MO 63105

Concordia Historical Institute
804 Seminary Place
St Louis, MO 63105
concordiahistoricalinstitute.org

Fenton Historical Society
Swanter House
One Church Street
Fenton, MO 63026
www.fentonhistory.com

Ferguson Historical Society
110 Church Street
St. Louis, MO 63135
www.fergusoncity.com

Historic Florissant
1067 Dunn Road
Florissant, MO 63031

Historical Society of University City
6701 Delmar Boulevard
University City, MO 63130
www.ucityhistory.org

Jennings Historical Society
8741 Jennings Station Road
Jennings, MO 63136

Kirkwood Historical Society
Mudd's Grove
302 W. Argonne Drive
Kirkwood, MO 63122
www.kirkwoodhistoricalsociety.com

Land Between the Rivers Historical Society
PO Box 200,
Portage des Sioux, MO 63373

Lewis and Clark Trail Heritage Foundation
www.lewisandclark.org

Old Trails Historical Society
Bacon Log Cabin
687 Henry Avenue
Ballwin, MO 63011
www.oldtrailshistoricalsociety.com

Overland Historical Society and Museum
2404 Gass Avenue
Overland, MO 63114
www.overlandhistoricalsociety.org

Sappington House Museum
1015 South Sappington Road
Crestwood, MO 63126
www.sappingtonhouse.org

St. Charles County Historical Society
Old Market House
101 South Main Street
St. Charles, MO 63301
www.scchs.org

St. Louis African American History and Genealogy Society
www.stl-aahgs.com

St. Louis Genealogical Society
#4 Sunnen Drive, Suite 140
St. Louis, MO 63143
www.stlgs.org

Sunset Hills Historical Society
www.sunset-hills.com/319/Historical-Society

Town & Country Historical Society
Longview Farm Park House
20 Roclare Lane
Town & Country, MO 63131
www.tandchs.org

Webster Groves Historical Society
Hawken House
1155 South Rock Hill Road
Webster Groves, MO 63119
www.historicwebster.org

BIBLIOGRAPHY

About St. Louis. "Bevo Mill." https://aboutstlouis.com.

————. "Calvary Cemetery." www.aboutstlouis.com/local/historic/calvary-cemetery.

————. "Soldiers Memorial Military Museum." https://aboutstlouis.com.

Academy of Science. www.academyofsciencestl.org.

Ambrose, Stephen E. *Undaunted Courage: Meriwether Lewis, Thomas Jefferson, and the Opening of the American West.* New York: Simon & Schuster, 1996.

Anheuser-Busch. "Building an American Icon." www.anheuser-busch.com/about/heritage.

Baldwin, Mike. "Paleontology: Mastodon State Historic Site." Memphis Archaeological and Geological Society. memphisgeology.org.

Basilica of St. Louis, King of France: The Old Cathedral. www.oldcathedralstl.org.

Bellefontaine Cemetery. www.bellefontainecemetery.org.

Browman, David L. "Cantonment Belle Fontaine 1805–1826: The First U.S. Fort West of the Mississippi River." Washington University Libraries. Julian Edison Department of Special Collections. 2018. https://aspace.wustl.edu/repositories/4/archival_objects/246415.

Bryan, William S., and Robert Rose. *A History of Pioneer Families of Missouri.* St. Louis, MO: Bryan, Brand & Company, 1876.

Burns, Adam. "St. Louis Union Station." American Rails. https://www.american-rails.com.

Campbell House Museum. www.campbellhousemuseum.org.

The Campbell House Museum: A Pictorial Souvenir. 5th ed. St. Louis, MO: Campbell House Foundation Inc., 2021.

Cass Gilbert Society. www.cassgilbertsociety.org.

Cathedral Basilica of St. Louis. www.cathedralstl.org.

Catholic Cemeteries. www.awaittheblessedhope.org.

Catholic News Agency. "A Sickness and a Silver Crown: How Saint Louis University Survived the Cholera Epidemic of 1849." March 25, 2020. www.catholicnewsagency.com.

Chapman, Carl H., and Eleanor F. Chapman. *Indians and Archaeology of Missouri*. Columbia: University of Missouri Press, 1983.

Charles, Ron. "Remodeled St. Louis Central Library Is a Marvel." *Washington Post*, March 29, 2013.

Chatillion-DeMenil Mansion. www.demenil.org.

Clevenger, Martha R., *"Indescribably Grand": Diaries and Letters from the 1904 World's Fair*. St. Louis: Missouri Historical Society Press, 1996.

Collins, Cynthia. "St. Louis Old Courthouse: Architectural Landmark and Historic Museum." *Guardian Liberty Voice*, July 19, 2014. https://guardianlv.com.

Compton Heights. www.comptonheights.org.

Designed By Frank Lloyd Wright. www.designedbyfranklloydwright.com.

Dickey, Michael. *People of the River's Mouth: In Search of the Missouria Indians*. Columbia: University of Missouri Press, 2011.

Erwin, James W. *St. Charles: A Brief History*. Charleston: History Press, 2017.

Erwin, Vicki Berger, and Justine Riggs. *Finally a Locally Produced Guidebook to St. Charles*. St. Louis, MO: Reedy Press, 2015.

The Fabulous Fox Theatre. www.fabulousfox.com.

Faherty, William Barnaby, SJ. *Henry Shaw: His Life and Legacies*. Columbia: University of Missouri Press, 1987.

Field House Museum. www.fieldhousemuseum.org.

Foley, William E. *The Genesis of Missouri: From Wilderness Outpost to Statehood*. Columbia: University of Missouri Press, 1989.

———. *A History of Missouri*. Vol. 1, *1673 to 1820*. Columbia: University of Missouri Press, 1999.

Forbes, Robert Pierce. *The Missouri Compromise and Its Aftermath: Slavery and the Meaning of America*. Chapel Hill: University of North Carolina Press, 2007.

Forest Park Forever. www.forestparkforever.org.

Forest Park Statues and Monuments. www.forestparkstatues.org.

Fox, Elana V. *Inside the World's Fair of 1904*. Vol. 1. St. Louis: 1st Books Library, 2003.

———. *Inside the World's Fair of 1904*. Vol. 2. St. Louis: 1ˢᵗ Books Library, 2003.

Fox, Timothy J., and Duane R. Sneddeker. *From the Palaces to the Pike. Visions of the 1904 World's Fair*. St. Louis: Missouri Historical Society Press, 1997.

Frank Lloyd Wright House in Ebsworth Park. www.ebsworthpark.org.

Frank Lloyd Wright Pappas House Foundation. www.flwpappashouse.org.

Frank Lloyd Wright Revival Initiative. www.flwrevivaliniative.org.

Gateway Arch National Park. www.gatewayarch.com.

Gilman, Carolyn. "*L'Annee de Coup*: The Battle of St. Louis, 1780, Part 1." *Missouri Historical Review* 103, no. 3 (April 2009), 133–45.

———. "*L'Annee de Coup*: The Battle of St. Louis, 1780, Part 2." *Missouri Historical Review* 103, no. 4 (July 2009), 195–211.

Goering, Karen. "Fighting for the Vision of Sacrifice at Soldiers Memorial." Missouri Historical Society. July 2, 2018. https://mohistory.org.

Grants Farm. www.grantsfarm.com.

Great Rivers Greenway. "Who Was Mary Meacham?" https://greatriversgreenway.org/mary-meachum.

Greene, Shawn Buchanan, ""Bombshell" Discovery Made at Hawken House." *Webster-Kirkwood Times*, February 14, 2022.

Hager, Ruth Ann (Abels). *Dred & Harriet Scott: Their Family Story*. St. Louis, MO: St. Louis County Library, 2010.

Hancock, Walker. "Oral History Interview with Walker Hancock, 1977 July 22–August 15." Smithsonian. Archives of American Art. https://www.aaa.si.edu.

Historical Marker Project. "St. Louis Arsenal: A State Divided: The Civil War in Missouri." https://historicalmarkerproject.com.

Holleman, Joe. "St. Louis' 3 Standpipe Towers Are Beautiful Both Inside and Out." *St. Louis Post-Dispatch*, July 7, 2016.

Hurt, R. Douglas. *Nathan Boone and the American Frontier*. Columbia: University of Missouri Press, 1998.

Iseminger, William. *Cahokia Mounds: America's First City* (Charleston: The History Press, 2010).

Jefferson Barracks POW-MIA Museum. "A Promise Made, a Promise Kept." https://jbpow-mia.org/about-us.

Jefferson Barracks Telephone Museum. "History." http://www.jbtelmuseum.org.

Jones, Jae. "Mary Meacham: Abolitionist Who Helped Those Enslaved Escape to Freedom." Black Then. May 6, 2021. https://blackthen.com.

Journals of the Lewis & Clark Expedition. https://lewisandclarkjournals.unl.edu.

Kavanaugh, Maureen O'Connor. *The Campbell Family of St. Louis*. St. Louis, MO: Campbell House Foundation, 2016.

Kienzle, Valerie Battle. *Walking Tour of St. Charles*. St. Louis, MO: Reedy Press, 2022.

Kloppe, Adam. "The Apotheosis of St. Louis." Missouri Historical Society. October 14, 2019. https://mohistory.org.

Koster, John. "Henri Chatillon's Heart of Lightness." HistoryNet. November 25, 2015. www.historynet.com.

Lacher, Julia. "Remember MLK's St. Louis Speech on the Future of Integration." Missouri Historical Society. January 13, 2021. https://mohistory.org.

Laumeier Sculpture Park. https://www.laumeiersculpturepark.org.

Lemp Mansion. https://lempmansion.com.

Lewis and Clark Boathouse. http://lewisandclarkboathouse.org.

Lewis and Clark State Historic Site. "Camp Dubois." https://campdubois.com.

Lothes, Scott. "John Walker Barriger: He Healed Railroads Using Pictures." *Trains Magazine*, June 14, 2012. www.trains.com.

Magic Chef Mansion. www.magicchefmansion.com.

McCandless, Perry. *A History of Missouri*. Vol. 2, *1820 to 1860*. Columbia: University of Missouri Press, 1972.

Minnelli, Vincent, dir. *Meet Me in St. Louis*. Beverly Hills, CA: Metro-Goldwyn-Mayer, 1944.

Missouri Botanical Garden. www.missouribotanicalgarden.org.

Missouri Civil War Museum. "Our Facility." https://mcwm.org.

Missouri Historical Society. "History of Soldiers Memorial Military Museum." https://mohistory.org.

———. "Quick Meal Stove." www.mohist.org.

Missouri Historical Society Library and Research Center. www.mohistory.org/library.

Missouri State Parks. "At First Missouri State Capitol State Historic Site, Launching Pad of Statehood." https://mostateparks.com.

———. "First Missouri State Capitol Historic Site." https://mostateparks.com.

———. "Mastodon State Historic Site." https://mostateparks.com.

———. "Scott Joplin House State Historic Site." https://mostateparks.com.

Morgan, Robert. *Boone: A Biography*. Chapel Hill, NC: Algonquin Books, 2007.

The Muny. www.muny.org.

Mueller, Carolyn. *Forest Park: A Walk Through History*. St. Louis, MO: Reedy Press, 2020.

Naffziger, Chris. "Adam Lemp's Riverfront Brewery Was the Birthplace of Lager Beer in St. Louis—and Perhaps America." *St. Louis Magazine*, August 9, 2017.

———. "The Genius of Julius Pitzman, Designer of St. Louis' Private Streets." *St. Louis Magazine*, October 8, 2014.

———. "How Adam Lemp Laid the Foundation of One of the Greatest Breweries in America." *St. Louis Magazine*, August 6, 2020.

———. "Unveiling the Real Johann Adam Lemp." *St. Louis Magazine*, August 2, 2017.

———. "Which of the Seven Wonders of the Ancient World Inspired St. Louis' Civil Courts Building? The Architects Stretched the Base of the Mausoleum of Halicarnassus to Towering Heights, Keeping the Ionic Colonnade and Egyptian Revival Stepped Pyramid." *St. Louis Magazine*, November 22, 2018.

National Blues Museum. https://nationalbluesmuseum.org.

National Museum of Transportation. https://tnmot.org.

National Park Service. "Camp Dubois," https://www.nps.gov/lecl/learn/historyculture/camp-dubois.htm

———. Gateway Arch. "Old Courthouse Architecture." https://www.nps.gov.

———. Gateway Arch. "Slave Sales." https://www.nps.gov.

———. "Hardscrabble: The House That Grant Built." https://www.nps.gov.

———. "Lewis & Clark National Historic Trail. Fort Belle Fontaine. " https://www.nps.gov.

———. "Missouri: The Shelley House." https://www.nps.gov.

———. Network to Freedom. "National Underground Railroad Network to Freedom." https://www.nps.gov.

———. "Ulysses S. Grant & White Haven." https://www.nps.gov.

———. "Why Is White Haven Painted Green?" https://www.nps.gov.

O'Neil, Tim. "Aug 1, 1943: Gliding Catastrophe Kills the St. Louis Mayor and Lambert Field's Co-Founder." *St. Louis Post-Dispatch*, August 1, 2022.

———. "A Look Back 60 Years Ago: The Day an Old Cathedral Secret Was Revealed." *St. Louis Post-Dispatch*, January 27, 2021.

———. "The Pope's Trip to St. Louis Was a Whirlwind 31-Hour Visit in 1999." *St. Louis Post-Dispatch*, January 26, 2022.

Parkman, Frances. *The Oregon Trail*. Oxford, UK: Oxford University Press, 2008.

Pauketat, Timothy M. *Cahokia: Ancient America's Great City on the Mississippi*. New York: Viking Press, 2009.

Pickard, Elizabeth. "Miss Nettie and the Lindberghs." Missouri Historical Society. August 11, 2019. https://mohistory.org.

———. "Miss Nettie's Ghost." Missouri Historical Society. March 2, 2016. https://mohistory.org.

———. "Miss Nettie's Notebooks and the MHS Story." Missouri Historical Society. August 11, 2016. https://mohistory.org.

Pittman, Rebecca F. *The History and Haunting of Lemp Mansion*. Wonderland Productions, 2015. Kindle Ed.

Pott Foundation. www.pottfoundation.org.

Preservation Journal. "The First State Capital." http://www.preservationjournal.org/properties/South/200-216/Booker.pdf.

Primm, James Neal. *Lion of the Valley: St. Louis, Missouri, 1764–1980*. 3rd ed. St. Louis: Missouri Historical Society Press, 2010.

Sacco, Nick. "The Contested Memories of General Nathaniel Lyon in St. Louis." *Journal of the Civil War Era*, May 28, 2019. https://www.journalofthecivilwarera.org.

Saint Louis Zoo. www.stlouiszoo.org.

Seppa, Nathan. "Ancient Cahokia: Metropolitan Life on the Mississippi." *Washington Post*, March 12, 1997.

Shepley, Carol Ferring. *Movers and Shakers Scalawags and Suffragettes*. St. Louis: Missouri History Museum, 2008.

Shoemaker, Floyd C. *Missouri's Struggle for Statehood, 1804–1821*. Jefferson City, MO: Hugh Stephens Printing Company, 1916.

Shrine of St. Joseph. www.shrineofstjoseph.org.

SmugMug. "Magic Chef Mansion Archives." www.magic-chef-mansion.smugmug.com.

Soulard Market. http://soulardmarketstl.com.

State Historical Society of Missouri. "Historic Missourians: Scott Joplin." https://historicmissourians.shsmo.org.

St. Charles County. "Historic Daniel Boone Home." https://www.sccmo.org.

St. Charles County Historical Society. www.scchs.org.

Stevens, Walter B. "Alexander McNair," *Missouri Historical Review* 27 (October 1922).

STL Beer. www.stlbeer.org.

STL News. "Calvary Cemetery." www.stl.news.

———. "National Blues Museum." https://www.stl.news.

St. Louis Art Museum. www.slam.org.

St. Louis County, Missouri. "Jefferson Barracks Park." https://stlouiscountymo.gov.

St. Louis, Missouri. "Forest Park." www.stlouis-mo.gov.

———. "Griot Museum of Black History and Culture." https://www.stlouis-mo.gov.

———. "Lyon Park." https://www.stlouis-mo.gov.

———. "On the Map: Mary Meacham Freedom Crossing." https://www.stlouis-mo.gov.

St. Louis Kaplan Feldman Holocaust Museum. www.stlholocaustmuseum.org.

St. Louis Parks, Recreation and Forestry. www.Stlouis-mo.gov/government/departments/parks.

St. Louis Public Library. "Central Library." www.central.slpl.org.

St. Louis Science Center. www.slsc.org.

St. Louis University. "Samuel Cupples House." https://www.slu.edu/cupples-house/index.php.

Tower Grove Park. www.towergrovepark.org/.

Trogdon, Jo Ann. *The Unknown Travels and Dubious Pursuits of William Clark*. Columbia: University of Missouri Press, 2015.

Truax, Mike. *The 1904 St. Louis World's Fair*. St. Louis, MO: 1904 World's Fair Society, 2017.

Union Station St. Louis. www.stlouisunionstation.com.

United Hebrew Congregation. "History." www.unitedhebrew.org/about/history.

United States Civil Rights Trail. "The Shelley House." https://civilrightstrail.com.

United States House of Representatives. "Edward Bates." http://history.house.gov.

U.S. Department of Veterans Affairs. "Jefferson Barracks National Cemetery." https://www.cem.va.gov.

U-S History.com. "Union Station St. Louis." www.u-s-history.com/pages/h3302.html.

Valone, Stephen J., ed. *Two Centuries of U.S. Foreign Policy: The Documentary Record*. Westport, CT: Praeger Publishers, 1995.

Wanko, Andrew. "Bevo Mill: From Anti-Prohibition Propaganda to a Neighborhood Landmark." Missouri Historical Society. https://mohistory.org/blog/bevo-mill, August 22, 2022.

Ware, Leland. "Contributions of Missouri's Black Lawyers to Securing Equal Justice: Shelley v. Kraemer." Missouri Bar. https://news.mobar.org.

Water Tower and Park Preservation Society. www.watertowerfoundation.org.

Webster Groves Historical Society. "Hawken House Museum." https://historicwebster.org.

Zimmerman, Lon. "The Architecture of Soldiers Memorial." Missouri Historical Society. March 5, 2021. https://mohistory.org.

ABOUT THE AUTHORS

Vicki Berger Erwin has been in the publishing industry for more than thirty years in various capacities, including sales, book distribution and as the owner of a bookstore in St. Charles, Missouri. She is the author of more than thirty books in varied genres: picture books, middle-grade mysteries and novels, local histories and true crime. She has an MFA in Writing Popular Fiction from Seton Hill University. James W. Erwin practiced law in St. Louis for thirty-seven years. He is the author of six books on local history. He has an MA in history and a law degree from the University of Missouri–Columbia. This is their third book together. They live in Crestwood, Missouri.